The Piper

at the Gates

of Dawn

Also available in this series

Forthcoming in this series

The Piper
at the Gates
of Dawn

John Cavanagh

continuum
NEW YORK · LONDON

2007

The Continuum International Publishing Group Inc
80 Maiden Lane, New York, NY 10038

The Continuum International Publishing Group Ltd
The Tower Building, 11 York Road, London SE1 7NX

www.continuumbooks.com

Printed in Canada

Library of Congress Cataloging-in-Publication Data

Cavanagh, John Eric, 1964-
The Piper at the gates of dawn / John Cavanagh.
p. cm. — (33 1/3)
ISBN 978-0-8264-1497-7 (pbk. : alk. paper)
1. Pink Floyd (Musical quartet). Piper at the gates of dawn.
I. Title. II. Series.
ML421.P6C38 2003
782.42166'092'2—dc21
2003008917

Contents

Acknowledgements

I'm indebted to the people who have spent time talking to me for this book. In alphabetical order they are: Kevin Ayers, Stewart Cruickshank, Mark Cunningham, Pete Drummond, Jenny Fabian, Duggie Fields, David Gale, Dave Harris, John "Hoppy" Hopkins, Jeff Jarratt, Peter Jenner, Andrew King, Arthur McWilliams, Nick Mason, Anna Murray-Greenwood, Keith Rowe, Matthew Scurfield, Vic Singh, Storm Thorgerson, Ken Townsend, Peter Whitehead and John Whiteley.

My thanks to Tim Chacksfield, Chris Charlesworth and Allan Rouse for contacts and, especially, to Alfie and Robert Wyatt who reversed the only negativity I met during the whole project.

Three books deserve a mention here, each one unique and all written by true Syd Barrett and Pink Floyd fans. David Parker burrowed deeper than the average mole into EMI's archives. His book *Random Precision* (published by Cherry Red) has gleaned improbable amounts of detail on just about every tape spool that ever rolled while Syd was in a studio, with and without the band. Glenn Povey and Ian Russell went to similar lengths for *In the Flesh* (Bloomsbury) in chronicling Pink Floyd's live shows and *Pink Floyd — The Press Reports (1966–1983)* by Vernon Fitch (CG Publishing) is an enjoyable read with a self-explanatory title.

I considered including the addresses of contributors' websites. On balance, this is not such a good idea: already during the time of writing, two of them have changed! Instead, I've put up a page at *www.phosphene. debrett.net/piper.htm* where I can give more detail and make sure the information is up to date.

The choice of album was mine. The idea that I should write this book was not. For that, I must credit and thank Neil Robertson, manager of the band Belle and Sebastian, and David Barker at Continuum.

1

The Run-in Groove

"That light you can see has taken 36 years to reach Earth," my brother told me as we looked towards Arcturus on a hot July night in 1975. I focused on the star and became mesmerized with the idea that the trajectory of this orangey-yellow glow across space had begun so long ago, or so it seemed to me as a ten-year-old.

Back inside our post-War end terrace house on the outskirts of Scotland's biggest city, Glasgow, I heard something on the radio that night which seemed as remote and other-worldly as Arcturus. To those who have grown up in the era of the CD and the easy availability of just about any sort of music from the back catalogue, I should explain something about 1975. As the glitter of glam rock became faded grandeur, 1975 was surely the year of the sharpest division between buyers of singles and buyers of albums. Novelty records, country dirges and weak imitations of reggae music filled the Top Forty and if anyone put out an exciting single (and the likes of Be Bop Deluxe and Brian Eno tried), then the chance of it getting anywhere was approximately nil. Many "albums bands" didn't even bother to issue singles at all. I mean bands like Led Zeppelin and, of course, Pink Floyd. I already loved The Floyd's *Meddle*, one of the first half dozen LPs I owned, but the thing I heard that night took me somewhere else entirely. Unlike anything I'd heard before, it was called 'Astronomy Domine'.

It was an event, a discovery. One moment I was looking at distant constellations, the next I was hearing a voice, like the sound of Apollo astronauts hailing the president from the moon, but more remote; a chugging incessant guitar; massive drums; a jagged bass riff and a song which name-checked planets and satellites, seemed to sweep the higher reaches of the infinite, then cascaded downwards towards "the icy waters underground". This was Pink Floyd? It didn't sound anything like *Dark Side of the Moon*, that was for sure. Then the DJ explained that this was from their first album, that Syd Barrett had fronted the band in those days and that he now lived in a cellar in Cambridge.

With my vivid imagination, I was off and running. He wasn't out in L.A. making dull AOR music and he wasn't a dead rock star, like Jimi Hendrix. He'd named this first Floyd album after a chapter in *The Wind in the Willows* by Kenneth Grahame (a favourite of mine!) and now he lived in an underground lair. Was he rock's answer to Mr. Badger, who lived right in the heart of the woods and preferred to see others before he was seen? This Syd Barrett was clearly unique and someone I wanted to know more about. The next day, I looked at the rack of Floyd LPs in Listen Records (the sort of shop where a picture of Zappa appeared on their carrier bags under the slogan FRANKLY CHEAPER!) and found *The Piper at the Gates of Dawn*. It was full price and I noticed that the more affordable *Relics* compilation album had 'See Emily Play' on it. That would do to start.

Relics, "a bizarre collection of antiques and curios", boasted a couple of amazing tracks from Pink Floyd's debut album: 'Interstellar Overdrive' and 'Bike'. Once I got into those, I had further incentive to own a copy of *Piper*. I'm quite sure that these sounds would have impacted on my world whenever I found them, but there was something about the arid musical landscape of the mid-70s which made them even more poignant. *Piper* has served as a form of musical escapism for many people across time, and an escape from 1975 was most welcome to me.

In time I learned more about Syd Barrett and realised that his journey back to a life in Cambridge had been a harrowing one. The stories of Syd's difficult latter days with Pink Floyd, his lifestyle and his solo albums have been told and re-told, sometimes with due regard for accuracy and sympathy for the subject and, sadly, on other occasions where the urge to print a spicy story overrides any other consideration. I am not a journalist. This fact was helpful when approaching those who had been stitched up by hungry hacks many times before, people like Duggie Fields, who still lives in a flat he once shared with Syd — his work space as an artist is the room which features on the sleeve of *The Madcap Laughs*. Over 30 years after Barrett left that address, Duggie still finds unexpected callers on his doorstep, people who are searching for . . . what? A rock 'n' roll myth or a man called Roger Barrett who has had nothing to do with the music industry for many years?

The Piper at the Gates of Dawn is a wondrous creation often seen through the distorted view of later events. These things have served to overshadow the achievement of The Pink Floyd on their debut album; an outstanding group performance; a milestone in record production; and something made in much happier circumstances than I had expected to find.

When I was, let's say, fourteen, I imagined myself going to Cambridge, meeting Mr. Barrett and becoming his friend. Of course, like many fans who had similar notions, I never did and wouldn't entertain the idea of disturbing him now . . . I'll leave that sort of crassness to the journalists who still bang on his door and snoop a photograph of him at the local shops or a view through his front window.

This is *not* another book about "mad Syd". This, instead, is a celebration of a moment when everything seemed possible, when creative worlds and forces converged, when an album spoke with an entirely new voice. "Such music I never dreamed of," as Rat said to Mole.

* * *

"We didn't start out trying to get anything new, it just entirely happened. We originally started as an R & B group," Roger Waters told a reporter from the Canadian Broadcasting Corporation (CBC), around the turn of the year 1966–7. Syd Barrett continued, "Sometimes we just let loose a bit and started hitting the guitar a bit harder and not worrying quite so much about the chords . . . " Roger: "It stopped being sort of third rate academic rock and started being intuitive groove." Syd: "It's free form."

By that time, Roger Keith "Syd" Barrett, Nicholas Berkeley Mason (known as "Nicky" at the time), George Roger Waters and Richard William Wright were only weeks away from signing a record deal with EMI and had rapidly built up a fan base for their live shows where improvised sound and light melded together. According to the (sadly nameless) girl who compiled the CBC feature, they had "stupefied audiences . . . [with] an array of equipment sadistically designed to shatter the strongest nerves. . . . " She pondered, "Is this the music destined to replace The Beatles? Are the melodic harmonies, poetic lyrics and soulful rhythms of today to be swept into the archives, totally undermined by a psychotic sweep of sound and visions such as this? Large pockets of enthusiasts from all over the country are determined that it shall, despite the powerful opposition of the majority of leading disc jockeys." On hearing this remarkable piece of prose, Canadian radio listeners could easily have been forgiven for thinking that Pink Floyd were causing anarchy on British streets, although listening now I ask myself why these powerful DJs would be so opposed to a band who had, as our trusty reporter says, "yet to make their debut on records"?

What The Pink Floyd were doing live was a unique evolution for a band who had started playing R & B covers. Two songs recorded in 1965 and widely circulated among Floyd fans illustrate their early sound with lead guitarist Bob Klose. 'Lucy Leave' is an original composition, with a strong vocal by Syd Barrett; the other title is the old Slim Harpo number 'I'm A King Bee', which The Rolling Stones covered. Bob appeared on *Crazy Diamond*, a BBC TV documentary devoted to Syd Barrett in 2001 and recalled: "You heard the early things, you thought maybe it's the Stones . . . and you recognise Syd's voice, but it's not Pink Floyd sound yet. It needed me to leave to do that. You know, that was quite an important step."

With Bob Klose off the scene (and pursuing a career as a photographer) Pink Floyd gradually moved away from jamming on 'Louie Louie' to create highly original new sounds. David Gale had grown up with Syd Barrett and Roger Waters in Cambridge: "I was present in Syd's bedroom in Hills Road, before we moved up to London, when he produced a Zippo lighter that he may well have got off an American serviceman and began running it up and down the neck of his guitar and saying 'What do you think of that?' He was not playing as if it were a bottleneck. In Cambridge people were already taking LSD in the nexus that circulated around Storm Thorgerson's house and Syd was among the people doing that. It may be that that made him impatient with doing Chuck Berry and Bo Diddley covers and made him experiment with other ways of getting sounds out of an electric guitar. He had two areas in which he could be experimental: guitar playing and painting. His painting had certain affinities with the pop art that Jim Dine was doing in the States, cloth appliquéd to canvas and heavily treated with oil paint."

Pink Floyd played at four events, a series of happenings called *The Spontaneous Underground*, held at the Marquee Club on Sunday afternoons between late February and early April 1966. John "Hoppy" Hopkins, photographer and key figure in the emergent counter culture, had his first experience of the band at one of these shows: "A lot of people who were around at that time were open to new or experimental sounds, pictures and movies, whatever was going down. They had a light show of sorts and the combination of that and the sound they were making really was very exciting. They were playing sheets of sound, sometimes similar to the way that AMM were treating the boundary between sound and music."

AMM were — and remain — a particularly innovative improv group with a floating lineup. Their first album *AMMUSIC 1966* was made by DNA, a small production company which involved both Hoppy and the man who was about to become Pink Floyd's co-manager, Peter Jenner (in partnership with his friend Andrew King). AMM took their cue from artists like Marcel Duchamp and the Dada movement, dispensing with conventional ideas of technique. Even today guitarist Keith Rowe neither rehearses nor tunes his guitar, preferring to apply different objects to the pickups and strings and use it as a sound generator.

Duchamp and Dada aside, it seems Pink Floyd's transformation had more practical roots. Bob Klose had been, in conventional terms, the most skilled musician in the lineup. Without him it was difficult to achieve a good standard repertoire for live shows. Better R & B bands were in abundance, so the competition was hot. Storm Thorgerson was one of the Cambridge boys who moved to London to study art. He told me: "When they were playing at The Marquee, they were booked in for longer than they had a set. In order to get paid properly, they had to play longer. They extended their songs in a rambling kind of fashion and it turned out very popular and got more people! They stopped doing blues and Syd was instrumental, literally, in turning them around."

John Whiteley, a former Buckingham Palace guardsman, was living at the same address as Syd in late 1966: "We went to see them at the Hornsey Art School and I'd expected a really super together band, but Syd was on stage shouting the chords to play to the other guys!" In July 1967, Peter Jenner talked to *Disc and Music Echo* magazine about the way Pink Floyd had arrived at their style: "My guess is that this was not even intentional. They are a lazy bunch and could never be bothered to practice, so they probably had to improvise to get away with it." Reflecting on their evolving style, Hoppy said, "I was trying to figure out what the pathways were and one of the key people in that was Joe Boyd. Joe was their first producer, he also produced the Incredible String Band and the recording that we made of AMM. The people in The Floyd were part of the receptive

This rare photo of Syd and Rick was taken by Graham Keen of International Times at the Hornsey College of Art on 18th November 1966.

participant audience for everything else that was going on, as we were to them. John Cage had come over round about that time and he had a show at the Saddle Theatre in Shaftesbury Avenue. Cage used silence as much as he used sound and we were all up for it, ready and excited, the place was full. The general context of people being ready for it, by some magical confluence of energies is what a lot of that rests on: all the cross-influences." Peter Jenner: "I think that things like AMM had an influence and, just generally, improvised music, whether it was jazz or whatever, but in songwriting, the influence was much more pop songs." Anna Murray was a close friend of Syd's. She says: "We were listening to the Beatles, Doors, Bob Dylan and then a lot of blues and jazz ... Miles Davis, Thelonious Monk, Charlie Parker ... "

"The next time I saw them, after *Spontaneous Underground*," says Hoppy, "was in Notting Hill. We called ourselves the London Free School. For my sins, I was the person paying for the printing of the newsletter and we were so disorganised that I was getting more and more in debt. I decided to hold a benefit at the local church hall [All Saints, Powis Gardens]. One of the bands that played was The Floyd and a few people turned up. The following week, The Floyd played again and a few more people turned up and by the third week it was quite obvious that we were sitting on some kind of tinderbox, because the queues were round the block! I have a muted memory of some sort of pleasure to do with having solved my financial problems, so the benefit was successful." Pink Floyd played ten London Free School shows between the end of September and late November 1966. Duggie Fields attended these events: "A group of friends was their audience first, then suddenly they got an enormous following within a very short space of time, shorter than it took for The Rolling Stones to happen."

Contemporary recordings of Pink Floyd speaking about their music are very rare, but they described their approach in that CBC interview. First, Syd: "In terms of construction, it's almost like jazz where you start off with a riff and then you improvise on that . . . " Roger cut in: "Where it differs from jazz is that if you're improvising around a jazz number and it's a sixteen bar number, you stick to sixteen bar choruses, you take sixteen bar solos, whereas with us, it starts and we may play three choruses of something that lasts for seventeen and a half bars each chorus and then it'll start happening and it'll stop happening when it stops happening and it may be four hundred and twenty three bars later, or it may be four!"

A set list from a Free School event on 14th October 1966 closed with 'Astronomy Domine' and also included 'The Gnome', 'Interstellar Overdrive', 'Stethoscope',

'Matilda Mother' and 'Pow R Toc H', six of the eleven titles which would end up on *The Piper at the Gates Of Dawn*. 'Lucy Leave' was still there; a couple of Bo Diddley numbers were the only non-original material played that night.

Writer Jenny Fabian's impression of the live Floyd experience was intense: "The first time they had less impact on me than later on, when I was on acid. It was at All Saints Hall and it was just — wow! — they're really weird and quite interesting looking." As the Free School events got busier, Hoppy knew it was time to step up a gear: "Joe Boyd said to me, 'If I can find a venue, why don't we take this West and run a club?', which was how UFO started and, of course, the first people to play there were The Pink Floyd." The opening night of UFO (pronounced "U-Fo" by the cognoscente) was two days before Christmas 1966 in the basement ballroom of The Blarney, an Irish pub on Tottenham Court Road. Jenny Fabian recalls: "The UFO things are imprinted forever on my consciousness. Kaftans, blobs . . . wonderful! You couldn't have asked for anything better than to be out of your head at UFO." Fittingly, for a club in an old ballroom, the audience was no longer static, as Duggie Fields remembers: "The first person I ever saw dancing to them was at All Saints Hall. All the projections and all the visuals were going on and everyone was laid back, except for one person who was dancing on his own and he was amazing! At UFO people would dance, that was just evolution." As Syd Barrett told the CBC reporter, "We play for people to dance to . . . they don't seem to dance much now, but that's the initial idea. So we play loudly and we're playing with electric guitars, so we're utilising all the volume and all the effects you can get." Roger Waters added: "But now we're trying to develop this by using the light." Jenny Fabian: "They did play music for our kind of dancing that was evolving. There was a very heavy rhythm thudding away, with these cosmic bleeps on top and then it would go off into something. If you're on acid, you just drift in that bit of music and gradually the rhythm seeps from underneath and you're taken over by the rhythm and it really used to enter into our bodies. Everybody danced, obviously plenty were flat on the floor! There were people floating around to it and people bopping to it quite nicely. I could do anything to their music."

The handful of UFO events crystallised a scene of cross-culture creativity, where Pink Floyd would appear with The Soft Machine, Marilyn Monroe films or AMM. Aside from UFO, the club circuit was vibrant: a look at Pink Floyd's live schedule from early 1967 finds them appearing, variously, with Cream; The Who; Alexis Korner; belly dancers, and . . . Tuppence the TV Dancer. In addition to music, the incursion of Beat writers meant that Pink Floyd might share a bill with, for example, the Scottish poet Alex Trocchi. This movement was propelled by a poetry event at the Albert Hall in 1965 (more of which later) and the efforts of people like Hoppy and Barry Miles to put more free thoughts into print. Jenny Fabian: "It was quite a London scene of underground thoughts and hedonism. People say now that it was a time when we were having all these thoughts of peace and love, but there was anarchy involved as well. The Floyd just fed that for us. They were opening the doors of musical perception and we felt they belonged to us. There were other people . . . there was Dylan, but he was far away and sort of God-like, The Beatles had evolved, but they didn't play live. So The Floyd were like our local consciousness come to life. It was as though they'd always been there . . . poets from the cosmos."

The Pink Floyd had gathered so much momentum with their live show that interest from record companies was inevitable. Both the band and their managers were fans of artists on the American label Elektra, founded in the 1950s by folk enthusiast and recording pioneer Jac Holzman, which had lately branched out from its New York H.Q. to sign some of the most exciting acts emerging on the West Coast. Peter Jenner: "We did audition for Jac Holzman, who turned us down. We did a showcase in the afternoon at The Marquee and he wasn't impressed. He did come more from a folky thing and I think it was a bit too loud and weird. If you think about the people he had — Arthur Lee and Love, proper songs and things, and The Doors were a band he would've found easier to relate to, whereas he had trouble later with The Stooges and the MC5 when David Anderle signed them. He couldn't quite handle that stuff. But we gave him all the waffle. He got the full ten minute rambles! I'm sure he thought, 'I'll never get this band on radio in America' — and we were probably out of tune."

Joe Boyd had worked for Elektra, branching out to form Witchseason Productions, which licensed his recordings of the Incredible String Band to Holzman's label. He hoped to sign The Floyd to Witchseason and was lining up a deal for releasing their music through Polydor. Meanwhile, Andrew King and Peter Jenner were shopping for an agent. "Richard Armitage was a big mainstream agent in Denmark Street and the people in his office wore morning suits," Andrew said, "then round the corner at 142 Charing Cross Road was Bryan Morrison with Steve O'Rourke and Tony Howard. He was booking The Pretty Things and all the bands that played at The Speakeasy, it was just groovier and the main reason for signing with Morrison was that he only wanted 10% commission and Armitage wanted to take 15%."

The Floyd didn't demo for EMI. Instead, they arrived with finished masters of two tracks which would form their first single. Joe Boyd produced these with engineer John Wood at his favoured studio, Sound Techniques, and it says a great deal for Boyd that he had anything to do with this session at all. With the realisation that he was losing the band, coupled with the knowledge that EMI had a strict policy regarding the use of "in-house" producers, he was creating a sweetener for a deal which was about to cut him out of the picture. Peter Jenner: "I was talking recently with Joe and I'd forgotten, but we completely stitched him up and fucked him off terribly. Apparently, the deal was all ready to go with Polydor and we backed away from it when EMI came in with a better deal with more money and better points. Polydor was, at that stage, a very new thing and we were advised by Bryan Morrison that we should go with EMI because of their distribution, they were much stronger in the market."

"More money" meant £5,000. When a decent wage in the U.K. was still less than £20 per week and £2,000 a year was a dream for most, it seemed a lot. The naïve Jenner and King were soon to find otherwise when they bought some new kit for the band. A Binson echo unit cost nearly £180 alone and, as these were the main effects used on both Syd's guitar and Rick's Farfisa Compact Duo organ, it didn't take long for the bill to add up to £2,000.

There was another reason for signing to EMI — perhaps the most important for the band: it was the home of The Beatles. "Wow, man!" says Peter Jenner. "You looked up the stairs at where The Beatles had their photo taken and then you went to Abbey Road where The Beatles were recording. Technical people wore brown coats, you had tea brought to you, one felt one was in a big family. It was a very comforting, institutional place. Altogether EMI was very reassuring, down to the commissionaires in uniform on the door, both at Manchester Square and Abbey Road. It was a bit like going to the BBC. There was Beecher Stevens, who signed the deal and then Norman [Smith] was our link with everything and subsequently, when records came out, we were involved with Roy Featherstone and, to some extent, Ron White and Ken East. We never, ever met [EMI chairman] Sir Joseph Lockwood. One *heard* Sir Joseph!"

*   *   *

Arnold Layne
Had a strange hobby
Collecting clothes
Moonshine washing line
They suit him fine!

The practice of hyping new artists on to the charts has been around as long as there have been charts. A shady area, yes, but commonplace. Even Jimi Hendrix's first single had a little "assistance" to help it on the way. In the mid-60s the BBC's monopoly on radio in the U.K. was challenged by offshore pirate ships, which operated for a prosperous couple of years until a legal loophole was closed. While the BBC made small concessions to the beat group boom with a couple of (admittedly excellent) shows, *Pick of the Pops* and *Saturday Club*, the pirates offered a constant stream of fresh pop sounds and made the BBC's *Light Programme* service sound very dated. Radio London pirate DJ Kenny Everett coined the word "Beeb" and portrayed the BBC as a stuffy maiden aunt and yet, while the BBC played Pink Floyd's song about a clothes fetishist, Radio London refused. "We spent a couple of hundred quid, which was quite a lot of money in those days," said Andrew King, "trying to buy it into the charts. The management did that, not EMI. It was the pirates that banned us. They were in the process of trying to get licenses and proving that they were respectable, so they were trying to be more 'Auntie Beeb-ish' than the Beeb. At the time I couldn't believe it. We were all reading William Burroughs and the idea that 'Arnold Layne' was naughty was weird to us!"

'Arnold Layne' b/w 'Candy and a Currant Bun' was a commercial breakthrough for Joe Boyd. It was also his last recording with Pink Floyd. Boyd's greatest skill as a producer lies in his ability to create an atmosphere which has allowed talents as diverse as Nick Drake, John Martyn and Vashti Bunyan to shine in the studio. His partnership with the outstanding engineer John Wood has endured and brought awards for their recent work with Toumani Diabate, but Peter Jenner is philosophical when he compares Boyd to the producer Pink Floyd were assigned by EMI, Norman Smith: "Syd did essentially write standard pop song structures, but then live they would improvise these long instrumental breaks. When Norman got hold of them, he thought this ain't gonna work and I don't think anybody minded because they all — especially Syd — listened to pop music. Live, they were all like 'Interstellar Overdrive'. Norman heard the songs and he made sure the songs came through. Joe would've had much more difficulty, I suspect, in getting them to chop the songs down in the studio, because he probably had much more of the status of a mate. I think Norman had that status of being the man from EMI, the man who'd worked with The Beatles, the guy who really knew what was going on. Joe had a lot of that, relatively, compared to us, but we instinctively felt he was one of us, whereas Norman was a real pro. He really knew what a hit record was."

*   *   *

My early memory of Norman, sorry "Hurricane", Smith is of him *having* hit records (like 'Don't Let It Die' in July 1971) rather than producing them. With bright floral shirts and a big moustache he looked to me like TV detective Jason King, as played by Peter Wyngarde, when I saw him on *Top of the Pops*. In the teenybop era of the Osmonds, Smith was an unlikely figure for chart success, but in his mid-late forties he enjoyed Top Five hits with annoyingly catchy songs and a rasping style, the vocal equivalent of Earl Bostic's saxophone playing. Peter Jenner had him marked out as "pretty groovy in an older way! He was a dapper dresser."

To get into EMI Studios as a recording assistant in 1959, Norman Smith had to shave six years off his age. Luckily his claim to be 28 (the age ceiling) was not challenged and he was one of a trio to be taken on from a pool of around 200 who had applied. His previous studio experience, allied to his ability as a player of brass, piano and drums carried him through to a world where strict guidelines governed the way records were made. Studios were places where "as live" performances were captured on tape. The idea of using any form of experimental recording technique was alien to most producers, as maverick engineer Joe Meek discovered. When he broke free of these formal constraints and created the unique sound world of 'Telstar', a global number one hit written and recorded in a small London flat, the industry was rattled.

The arrival of another force was about to change the rules completely and Norman Smith was with it from the beginning. Jeff Jarratt, who began working at EMI in autumn 1966 (and was tape op. on most of the *Piper* sessions) explains: "Norman was the engineer on Beatles recordings from when they first started at Abbey Road. He did their audition and followed through, working with them for several albums. He was well versed in the sort of lateral thinking one had to have if you were working with The Beatles. They would always be coming up with new ideas. In their own way, The Floyd had that same thirst for trying to do things which were a little different from anything going on at the time: he was the right person to have around, to be open-minded about how you could re-think the normal recording process." Peter Jenner: "We were the first pop band that EMI signed to an album deal. That was part of the thing we were holding out for, because we wanted to do our long rambles, we wanted to be free, man! We didn't want to be held down, man! But I think Norman quietly and craftily got them to record a pop album." Andrew King: "He was not at all conservative; he never said 'You can't do that because that's not the way we do things'. Norman did it with a very light hand. [He] didn't tell them how they had to do it. They'd say what they wanted to do and he enabled them to do what they wanted."

Norman Smith chooses not to discuss his work with Pink Floyd these days, which is a great pity as his early involvement with the band has suffered some revisionism, becoming tarnished by events further down the line. When I started on this book, I viewed Smith as a jazz snob, someone who was not in tune with the band. I imagined that *Piper* was good in spite of him. An oft-quoted line from a 1973 edition of *ZigZag* magazine fuelled this perception: Roger Waters described 'Apples and Oranges' (a single from late 1967) as "a fucking good song . . . destroyed by the production". My impression was quite clearly wrong. Peter Jenner offered his perspective: "It all became more fraught later on, after 'See Emily Play'. From there on in the pressure built up. . . . We need another hit, Syd, we need a new single and then when Syd had gone it all became much, much more difficult. I recall *Piper at the Gates of Dawn* being really exciting and fun. Hard work, but positive. I can't remember people storming out. Being uptight or worried was definitely something which came subsequently."

Waters wasn't the only one with a few sharp words. Smith talked about his career to *Studio Sound* magazine for their May 1998 issue: "I can't in all honesty say that the music meant anything at all to me. In fact, I could barely call it music, given my background as a jazz musician and the musical experience that I'd had with The Beatles. After all, with The Beatles we're talking about something really melodic, whereas with Pink Floyd, bless them, I can't really say the same thing for the majority of their material. A mood creation through sound is the best way that I could describe The Floyd. . . Nevertheless, we got along as well as anybody could with Syd Barrett. He really was in control. He was the only one doing any writing, he was the only one who I, as a producer, had to convince if I had any ideas, but the trouble with Syd was that he would agree with almost everything I said and then go back in and do exactly the same bloody thing again. I was really getting nowhere."

While that's certainly true of later sessions, it was not the case with the *Piper* recordings. Jeff Jarratt: "When I was asked to do the album, I went down to see them at the Regent Polytechnic, to know what it was all about before we started working and their performance on stage was quite fantastic. It was literally just a matter of capturing that when they came into the studio. Sure, they would do a few takes, but that's normal. They were extremely efficient. Most of what you hear on that album was done on the basic recording. Obviously, there would be some overdubs." The session sheets for all the early Floyd work with Norman Smith were unearthed by David Parker for his book *Random Precision* and the facts are clear: two songs on *Piper* needed only a single take to achieve a master recording.

Jeff Jarratt's credits range from The Beatles to Barbra Streisand. He describes Norman Smith as "absolutely fantastic. Nobody knew how the studio worked better than him . . . one of the best people I've ever worked with." In an internet interview with Richie Unterberger, Phil May of The Pretty Things said, "If there hadn't been Norman Smith, The Floyd wouldn't have been able to develop what they were trying to do. There was nobody with ears like Norman." Nick Mason put the situation in context: "Our split with Norman came further down the line when it became apparent that he would've liked to have stuck with what one might call the classic pop music style and length and so on. Norman felt, very strongly, that that's how records should be made. I think he was less interested in the ramblings of the band. To some extent history proved him wrong, but at the time it was the recordings that gave us some popularity. We were popular at the UFO and the few underground clubs, but basically our long improvisations didn't work that well when we went up to the North, or indeed further East or West. He was a lovely man and I was very fond of him. We, more or less, managed to part as friends rather than any other way, which is nice."

The other key member of the production team was the late Peter Bown. "He started off as a classical engineer," said Jeff Jarratt, "but he crossed over all the different genres that came into the studio. His personality was such that he lived for recording and was a fun person to be around." Andrew King recalled: "He said the faders were wearing out the ends of his fingers and he'd sit at the desk painting the ends of his fingers with this little pot of plastic skin which you'd put on sores and cracks." Ken Townsend, fondly remembered for his time as manager of Abbey Road, says Peter had a crew-cut hairstyle and "nearly married ['50's singing star] Ruby Murray, but his mother didn't approve, then he went a bit 'the other way' later on." The straight side of Mr. Bown wasn't obvious to Peter Jenner: "He was as bent as a nine bob note! So quite florid, but he was sweet and very supportive. I think he liked the band and would help them along, but every now and then the eyebrows would raise — 'Oh my God, what are they doing now?' sort of thing. He helped hold the sound together. It was a good team."

While it was alright for Syd Barrett to kick off his shoes in EMI studio 3, it wasn't so free and easy for employees like Jeff Jarratt: "Technical chaps always wore white coats on sessions and engineers had to wear ties, which was pretty silly. I got sent home one day for not wearing a tie!" Nick Mason recalled the session structure: "They were fairly formalised, EMI had specific three hour sessions, nine until twelve or two until five. We might do two sessions in a day, or go from afternoon to evening and the evening ones would run late, but it wouldn't be unheard of for us to be out of there at five to make way for someone else." Jeff Jarratt: "The amazing thing about working at Abbey Road was that, in the morning, you could be working with Sir Adrian Boult, Sir John Barbirolli or Otto Klemperer and then Victor Sylvester and his ballroom band in the afternoon and in the evening you could be doing The Beatles or The Pink Floyd. We used to finish at three or four in the morning and you could be back in there at a quarter to ten for a session the next morning and I did this seven days a week for several years!"

It's often assumed that The Beatles were the first artists to record through the night and that late sessions were a bonanza for producers and engineers. Ken Townsend clarified that point: "The very first person to work late night was Adam Faith. I did midnight to three a.m. sessions with him in 1958–59 when John Barry was the musical director. The Musicians Union specified an excessive payment if you worked beyond, say, ten o'clock at night [for artists]. Nothing to do with studio staff: they got flat rate."

2

Side One

A cynic might say that Norman Smith was making up for those flat rate late nights by using a whole four hour session on the introductory tape for 'Astronomy Domine', but as a mood setter for the album it was undeniably time well spent. The disembodied, cut-up voice is Peter Jenner's: "I was just there and they wanted another voice, I guess I had a posh voice or something. When they did it live someone had to have a megaphone and then they all had to start playing. I just read some stuff through the megaphone." Jenner recalls an *Observers Book of Planets*, which Syd carried around with him and consulted whilst writing 'Astronomy Domine'. On record, layers of the megaphone voice, fused together, just on the verge of perception, fade in heralding Syd's Telecaster, a pulse on one key from Rick's Farfisa Compact Duo (except when he accidentally strikes the adjacent note!) — a mock Morse message — then the deep bass of Roger's Rickenbacker 4001 is reinforced by a drum sound which is far removed from the small kit sonorities typical of most pop records.

Nick Mason: "That was recorded using a Premier Kit. It was a double bass-drum thing, because I'd been turned on by seeing Ginger Baker and Cream probably about six months before we were recording that. It's quite a live drum sound, that's the thing about it. I don't think I had very much input into the drum sound at that time, I wouldn't have known very much about it. It was all down to Norman Smith producing and Pete Bown's engineering." Andrew King: "I don't think you'll ever see an engineer do this these days . . . Pete would go out into the studio, listen to them running through the numbers, listen to what Nick's drums sounded like, for instance, and then go back and do everything he could to recreate that. It was based on the tradition of engineering classical music at Abbey Road: to reproduce, in the control room, the sound that was being made in the studio and that's why it sounds so fresh and live."

As the opener on a debut album, 'Astronomy Domine' sets an incredibly high standard, but the feeling is carried throughout the ten tracks which follow. Pink Floyd's favourite effects unit, the Binson Echorec with its multiple tape heads, overloaded valve electronics and winking green "magic eye" level indicator, swirls and pulses through the elemental images as Syd and Rick sing of subterranean icy waters and remote space. Peter Jenner: "The first time I saw them at the Marquee I remember walking round the stage trying to work out where the noise was coming from: Rick or Syd? Syd was playing these really long repeated things on his Binson Echorec and Rick, too, had an Echorec so there was all this sustain going." Nick Mason: "At the time it was one of the echo units that was available from most of the music shops. It had all sorts of mechanical problems, but it's a fantastic piece of kit. They look as though they'd be most comfortable in the science museum! They can make almost any instrument sound as if it's been recorded by Thomas Edison himself, in terms of the way you get a build-up of white noise, but that's part of the attraction of it."

Pink Floyd delivered something new, a cohesive amalgam of melody, discord and abstract sound unlike anything that went before, so it seems appropriate that 'Astronomy Domine' should refer to the comic hero Dan Dare, Pilot of the Future.

*   *   *

In May 1967 *Trend*, a magazine aimed at teenage girls, ran a photo feature on Pink Floyd called "The Pink and Their Purple Door". It wasn't the only piece to cast the band as four lads sharing a flat in London's Cambridge Circus with — you've guessed it — a purple door. Perhaps EMI's marketing people had The Monkees in mind? The reality was a far more complex, shifting scene and, at that stage, an address associated with The Floyd usually meant the place where Syd lived. As Nick Mason says: "Roger, Richard and I were living with respective girlfriends."

Syd Barrett migrated to London with Cambridge schoolfriend David Gale: "Syd and I had a mattress each on either side of a small room in a dreadful house on Tottenham Street, near Heal's on Tottenham Court Road. It was a motley collection of people — ageing alcoholics, bums, peanut salesmen and beatniks room by room in a couple of linked houses. [Then] we moved down to Earlham Street." Duggie Fields: "There's a group of flats I connect with The Floyd; Earlham St, which would be the Cambridge Circus one (that was the early hotbed of Peter Wynne Wilson's light shows); Cromwell Road; then Egerton Court."

Storm Thorgerson: "I stayed in 2 Earlham Street, right on the corner of Cambridge Circus, for about three months. Syd was two floors down in a four storey house. It was quite a narrow house, very narrow staircase." John Whiteley lived there for about five years, on and off. Of his second stint, he says: "The guy who rented the house was called Jean Simone Kaminsky, an outrageous character. He was on the run from the French army. He was helped by an MP and he came to a 'safe house' in Cambridge next door to Matthew Scurfield." Kaminsky made the move to London, found work at the BBC and, Whiteley says, "through Jean Simone, Ponji [whose full name was John Paul Robinson] came to live in Earlham Street, then I met them all — Storm, Aubrey Powell (Po), a lot of The Floyd . . . "

Matthew Scurfield became part of the scene at the house in Earlham Street, initially through visits to Ponji, his half brother: "It had a tongue and groove wooden ceiling and you slightly felt there could be cockroaches, but you tried not to notice that. Jean Simone was involved in putting intellectual porno books together . . . " David Gale takes up the story: "One of his printing presses had short-circuited and burnt the flat down and the fire brigade noticed there were some moist pornographic novels to be found in the general detritus and called the cops. The cops then made it impossible for Jean to ever go home again." Earlham Street was also home to Anna Murray: "Jean Simone managed to escape through the flames in his underpants and ran up the road where there was a fire station." Anna remembers "sacks of pornography lying around the place: a complete nightmare! We spent a whole night driving around Hampstead dumping it in people's gardens so the cops wouldn't find it!" "Everyone was very cool up to a point," says Matthew, "but suddenly all that 60s cool went out the window . . . my brother even had to jump out the window!"

"It was Peter Wynne Wilson who actually pioneered some of the early projection technology for The Pink Floyd," David Gale says. "It was Pete, for example, who stretched a condom over a wire frame and then dropped oil paint onto it and tapped it with his fingers whilst shining a powerful light through it in order to get the first oil slide effect. It was also Pete who had the idea of taking a pair of welding goggles and removing the dark glass, replacing it with clear glass and Aralditing two glass prisms onto the front and making 'cosmo-nocles' — the word was my invention — and I remember being led by Pete Wynne-Wilson down Charing Cross Road wearing his cosmonocles and the world didn't half look weird because you were seeing it prismatised." John Whiteley remembered another device which used a stretched condom with a mirror attached to it. This could vibrate in time to the music, allowing the mirror to reflect a dancing rhythmic pulse of light.

Syd moved from Earlham St. to 101 Cromwell Road, where Duggie Fields lived. Duggie recalls light shows as part of the scene there 'when The Floyd were rehears-ing, or perhaps even when they weren't. We had a two floor, seven room flat. [1965 movie] *The Knack* was the influence on painting the first floor living room white: white walls, white floor. We were very into the cinema; late night cinemas; all night cinemas; and one or two cinemas where you'd walk in and the whole place was stoned! Minimum of nine people living there, I don't know how many people stayed the night during the week, but at weekends it was uncountable. Sometimes there'd be some fabulous strangers and sometimes just . . . strangers! We were on the top floors. On the floor below was a man who lived on his own and then took in lodgers from our group, but he was very, very conventional and he was always taking out the fuses to plunge us into darkness because of the noise. Then on the floor below that was the team from Cambridge, some of whom moved upstairs to our flat, so it was two very integrated flats, but with a gap in the middle."

"The people on the floor below had a society to legalise marijuana, which had a public meeting, got raided and was in the local paper with blacked out photographs of teenagers smoking marijuana after midnight. The 'after midnight' was very significant! At the biggest meeting they had, I remember Nico was there. I remember Yoko Ono coming round to the flat and me staying upstairs and refusing to come downstairs and be interested in her in the slightest. I was asked if I wanted to be in her *Bottoms* movie. I thought no, but now I wish I had . . . John Mayall moved into the flat for maybe a week or two. There was a musical contingent in and out of the flat that wasn't just The Pink Floyd."

"We never had any money, but we did seem to be able to get taxis. I remember the number of times I got into a taxi and I'd say '101' and they'd say 'Cromwell Road?' and they'd see by the way we looked that that was where we came from. Tourism in London didn't exist like it does now. The whole 'Swinging London' thing was starting to happen in the media and one would get photographed in the street quite often. Then we started getting American girls following us into the flat, just because of the way we looked. This was quite regular."

As manufacturers latched onto these "weird" styles, the innovators were scathing, as Jenny Fabian remembers: "When a hippy fashion developed, none of us wore it. That was for the plastic hippies and the weekend hippies. The true underground were always one step either ahead or behind, never in time." Even in such a distinctive scene, Pink Floyd were unmistakable, as Jenny says: "They were dressed like 18th century fops. They weren't dressed in the clothes of the time outside of the acid consciousness. We were all dressing outside time: girls were either wearing ethnic clothes or going back in time to look like 40s film stars."

Of the trio of addresses that Duggie associates with Pink Floyd, Egerton Court is post-*Piper*, but it's worth a brief mention here. Storm Thorgerson described it as "a bit of a dump, but a great flat, on a corner in South Ken[sington] just opposite the tube, right in the middle of activity, five minutes from Hyde Park and near our college. It was a period block with great tall ceilings and it had a big, wide circular stairway and an old 30s lift that went up the middle of the stairway." Roman Polanski had filmed these features in 1965 for *Repulsion*, starring Catherine Deneuve.

As a footnote to life in Cromwell Road, Duggie told me: "I was having an exhibition at a gallery and the dealer said to me, 'By the way, I used to live in Cromwell Rd, 101.' He said he lived there for six weeks in the summer of 1967. I don't think I'd ever laid eyes on him. He said, no, he never came upstairs, because he was too in awe of Syd!"

"People in Haight Ashbury probably thought that San Francisco was the centre of the world," says Storm. "They may have had the Grateful Dead, they may have had Jefferson Airplane and they may even have had Captain Beefheart . . . but they were wrong, of course!"

* * *

Alongside the ebb and flow of interesting people in Pink Floyd's circle came a strong current of ideas, many of which were rapidly forgotten. One of these was a film on the life of a cat called *Percy the Ratcatcher*. Although this was mentioned in the music papers, no one I've spoken to can remember it. However, the song of the same title would evolve, during recording, into 'Lucifer Sam', the second track on *Piper*.

Nick Mason remembers the process as ideas became album tracks: "There's a difference between a number of them. Some would arrive as songs absolutely ready to play and we would simply learn them because Syd had already worked them out and other songs would be developed in the studio or, indeed, have arrangements devised for them by Norman. The ones that were played live were the ones that were more developed by the band, which would be things like 'Astronomy Domine' and, obviously, 'Interstellar Overdrive'. Things like 'Chapter 24' . . . a lot of those things would come as a song played on the guitar, which was then developed into keyboard parts and then what the solos might do (or not) and that's when, particularly, Norman would get involved in changing the dynamic of the song."

Dave Harris was an EMI studio manager at the time, who would set up the studio before each session began. He spoke of the dynamic within the production team: "Norman Smith never seemed to panic; he was always cool; he always had a great sense of humour. Peter Bown used to panic like mad sometimes and [imitates wheezing sound] he'd blow his cigarette ash all over!

As an engineer, he was a perfectionist. They *really* worked together."

In recording terms, 'Lucifer Sam' was the most complex item on the album. After the basic track was put down on April 12th, it was revisited for overdubs at five sessions before a final mixdown at the end of June. This would have been unthinkable when groups were expected to cut an album in a day, but the climate was changing. "*Piper* was recorded in what one might call the old fashioned way: rather quickly," says Nick Mason. "As time went by we started spending longer and longer. The Beatles were recording *Sergeant Pepper* and EMI were susceptible to the idea of spending a lot more time in the studio, but we were still, quite often, using afternoon sessions and then actually going and doing gigs in the evening. We didn't know any better in terms of how to really burn time!"

For example, a 2.30–6.30pm studio booking to overdub maraccas, organ and bowed bass to what was still known as 'Percy' was followed by a quick trip to Essex to play the Tilbury Railway Club. As for the bowed bass, Nick says: "It wasn't as though this was a total breakthrough, that no one had done it before. It was like a number of things . . . you see someone doing it and, you know, Roger obviously thought 'I could do that' so that was brought on board."

Waters' bass sound is an exotic highlight within a richly textured mix as several layers of keyboard and assorted percussion fuse round the descending/ascending minor key theme. It's a slightly dark mood, more reminiscent to me of Link Wray than the music of The Ventures, which is sometimes attributed as an influence. As Syd Barrett sings,

> *Night prowling sifting sand*
> *Padding around on the ground*
> *He'll be found*
> *When you're around*

syllables and notes flow together in close rhythmic unison. "Syd's lyrics were quite whimsical," says Storm Thorgerson, "a cross of mysticism with various fairy tales and magical creatures. They certainly had a very distinctive cadence, which often didn't mean very much, even to Syd. He wasn't so interested in the meaning, he was interested in the sound." Jenny Fabian: "Syd captured the feeling of our consciousness with his very strange words. They weren't the words you heard in normal pop songs . . . unicorns, visions from Arcadia, chings, all sorts of things that we were all interested in." All of those things and more but, conspicuously, no mention of that favoured pop song theme: love. Whilst the love of elemental nature and space is here, the only mention of anything that can be tied to a personal relationship on the entire album lies within 'Lucifer Sam'.

> *Jennifer Gentle you're a witch*
> *You're the left side*
> *He's the right side oh no*

Duggie Fields contemplated the reference: "Jennifer Gentle . . . not Jenny Fabian — Jenny Spires, definitely, who came down to London as a model and at the time she was very close to Lindsay Corner. Both girls went out with Syd. Jenny was breathtakingly gorgeous."

Barrett's solo work was much more raw and personal. For his songs on *Piper*, mysticism and abstract characters were dominant. As Storm Thorgerson says, "What doesn't seem to infuse the lyrics is his desire for a good time and chasing girls. I think there were some references to psychology, but not a lot; separation images; twins; the other side of something; the reverse are, I think, mentioned or implied in various cases. There's not a lot of politics — if any — very little sex, so there's quite an interesting psychological profile that you could draw from all of this, which you don't need me for — ha!"

Listen and theorise if you feel the need. I don't intend to impute any crass notions of Syd's psyche in print.

After all, what do any of us really know? As the song says, "That cat's something I can't explain."

*   *   *

"The Pink Floyd group specialise in 'psychedelic music', which is designed to illustrate LSD experiences." That line ran beneath a shot of Rick, Roger, Nick and Syd looking the picture of innocence amidst their instruments in Britain's Sunday tabloid paper *The News of the World*, only nine days before the band's first recording session at Abbey Road. This thrilling exposé (the *NOTW* still specialises in them!), headlined "Pop songs and the cult of LSD", was "Continuing the investigation that has set Britain talking, POP STARS AND DRUGS", and carried a print of the masthead for "The PSYCHEDELIC EXPERIENCE, a manual based on *The Tibetan book of the Dead*", a photo of Timothy Leary ("words and phrases from the drug prophet's book are being used in today's pop records") and a story which ran: "It is impossible to exaggerate the hold which the hallucination drug LSD has gained on the pop world during the past year, or the speed with which it is becoming 'fashionable' among the beat groups' teenage fans. LSD groups even have their own newspaper and literally dozens of magazines and pamphlets imported from the United States extol the virtues of taking the drug as a 'way of life.' The influence of the drug has taken Tin Pan Alley, headquarters of Britain's music publishing, by storm."

The newspaper acted as catalyst to the notorious drug bust at Redlands, Keith Richards' Sussex home, on February 12th 1967 when Keith, Mick Jagger and art dealer Robert Fraser were arrested. Of those *NOTW* articles, Nick Mason recalls: "They got it wrong — they said we called ourselves social deviants — we didn't: that was Mick Farren's support band" [who were actually called The Social Deviants].

While Syd's acid consumption is the stuff of legend, Roger, Nick and Rick were remarkably straight. Their drug of choice was more likely to be a pint at the local pub. Luckily for all concerned, the mud didn't stick. Peter Jenner: "With hindsight I think, fucking hell, how did we get away with this when you see the hysteria that goes down when someone does some drugs, even now? EMI did a fantastic job. We could've been pursued to death. I mean that, for Christ's sake, was the time when Mick Jagger was put in jail. I was working at the LSE [the London School of Economics, a place which was viewed as a hotbed of radical opinion] and was managing this band which was supposedly encouraging people to take acid, mind-altering substances. It could've ricocheted on me; it could've ricocheted very nastily on the band when you think about it. There we were quite clearly simulating drug experiences, that's part of what we were doing. Hey, when you take a trip, you hear sounds like this and then we played it to them. There was all sorts of stuff in our publicity about mind expanding and things like that. It really helped that we were on a big label. I mean, EMI wouldn't have anything to do with drugs — hey, these guys make weapons for our boys! EMI was like the BBC, it was like the government or the Civil Service. I think if we'd been with Elektra or Polydor it would've been much more difficult. Elektra would've been a dodgy little American company and Polydor would be the damned Huns! You can imagine . . . "

The less fortunate were in for a hard time. Hoppy fell foul of the authorities' interest in the underground and was sentenced to nine months in Wormwood Scrubs for possession of a small quantity of pot, a term which began the day *Sergeant Pepper* hit the shops: "I was in jail when [*Piper*] was released, so I never got to hear it as a new release. In the grimy, grey and medieval workshops, the one bright note was that they had this radio station over the PA the whole time and when *Sergeant Pepper* was released, they kept playing it and it was absolutely brilliant! The world is full of contradictions and the fact that they didn't censor the music coming over the radio is a happy little contradiction. They used to censor the mail absurdly: if someone would send me a psychedelic picture, then the chances are that it wouldn't get through, because it looked so weird they felt perhaps it was laced with acid or something. They didn't have a clue . . . the place to put acid is under the postage stamp!"

*　　*　　*

Although *The News of the World* article did not say overtly that Pink Floyd lyrics contained elements of Dr. Leary's words, the implication was clear. It was, of course, nonsense: the merry pranksters who influenced Syd Barrett's songs were not the American turn-on merchants. Andrew King says the original version of 'Matilda Mother' quoted words by Hilaire Belloc:

> *There was a boy whose name was Jim*
> *His friends were very good to him*
> *They gave him tea and toast and jam*
> *And slices of delicious ham*
> *Oh oh mother*
> *Tell me more*

Andrew adds: "The iambic beat of Belloc totally fits the metre of the song. The Belloc estate weren't keen at all, so Syd replaced the extracts. It was a pure copyright issue." Listening to 'Matilda Mother' — the verses sung on record by Rick Wright — I'm thankful that the heirs of Hilaire inadvertently forced Syd Barrett to write his own words, which are much more attuned to the atmosphere of the music:

> *There was a king who ruled the land*
> *His majesty was in command*
> *With silver eyes*
> *The scarlet eagle*
> *Showered silver on the people*
> *Oh mother . . .*

Duggie Fields reflected on shared interests whilst listening to 'Matilda Mother': "*Grimm's Fairy Tales* were around; *The Hobbit* and *Lord of the Rings*; Carlos Castaneda's *Teachings of Don Juan*; Aldous Huxley; all sorts of science fiction (I remember reading [Robert Heinlein's] *Stranger in a Strange Land* in Cromwell Road, so Syd would probably have read that at the same time); any mythological stories all mixed up with a bit of Dada. Yoko Ono's *Grapefruit* book was around; Burroughs; French literature . . . Cocteau. As a group, we'd all read the same books, we all turned each other on to books continuously. Syd had Aleister Crowley, a first edition of *Moonchild*. That was the first time I'd come across Crowley, who was a very underground cult figure. He had the *I-Ching* around 1966. I can't think of any music that would've been the background for making lyrics like this. It was coming from what he was reading. I had a wall of Marvel comics at Cromwell Road. I used to pin them up and people would just come and take them. Whether we have any Marvel comics influence in here . . . I'm sure we do."

The Piper at the Gates of Dawn was recorded in Studio 3 at Abbey Road (or, more accurately, EMI Studios: it only became known as Abbey Road thanks to The Beatles' 1969 LP, not before it) using Studer J37's, the same exceptionally high quality valve tape machines running next door in Studio 2 for *Sergeant Pepper*. Although eight track recording had been in use in the States for several years, it wasn't until 1968 that the first eight tracks appeared in U.K. studios, so four track recording onto one inch wide tape was still the state of the art in 1967.

When I began work on this book I hoped that I would be able to recapture the atmosphere of the sessions by hearing these master reels. It was a big disappointment to find that, aside from one spool which remains in EMI's tape library — the result of Pink Floyd's first session for *Piper*, containing their half dozen shots at 'Matilda Mother' — the masters were most likely bulk-erased, put in fresh boxes and used again. The large, heavy spools were considered too precious to edit, so compiling a finished track from two or more different takes was something which would happen only after a 'reduction' had been made. Pre-planning by the production team was essential, as the only way to add extra sounds was to mix the initial four tracks down (hence 'reduction') and 'bounce' this to another machine, freeing up space for fresh recordings.

Peter Jenner spoke of the mastery of engineers at EMI who "could edit in the middle of a violin sustain and you'd never hear it", and whilst that was often true, 'Matilda Mother' is one place on *Piper* where there are audible joins. Given the complexity of material and the processes involved, it's amazing that there weren't many more obvious splices.

Although 'Matilda Mother' was not a new number, it was developed in the studio. Peter Jenner says that, when it came to structure and harmony, "Norman Smith was proactive; he did have a lot of influence." Nick Mason agrees: "Oh, very much so! In fact, every now and again you can hear Norman singing on the record as part of the harmony group — I'm sure he's on there!" Norman would illustrate his ideas on harmony at the studio piano and the richness of that vocal blend really shines on 'Matilda Mother'.

Sung from a young child's perspective, 'Matilda' is filled with magical other-worldly images and the slightly impatient longing for more. Barrett's lines about "doll's house darkness" and "fairy stories held me high on clouds of sunlight floating by" seem reflective of his own childhood. Matthew Scurfield remembers visiting Syd's family home: "It was quite a dark house, very womb-y, in a funny kind of way. In Cambridge, the word was everything: if you had a light, it didn't matter whether there was a window, so long as you could read your book! If you're brought up in an academic world, you tend to create your own space as a child. The imaginary world is your saving grace."

Just before Syd's sixteenth birthday his father, Max Barrett, died. Storm Thorgerson says: "His mother was over motherly, too lenient by half as a result of it." The lack of father figures was surely a bond between some of Syd's Cambridge friends: Roger Waters and Ponji Robinson's fathers were killed in World War II, and Storm's lived in another part of England. There's an added poignancy to 'Matilda' when one considers Barrett's return to his mother Winifred and the family home in later, darker times.

*   *   *

"The Floyd are one of the few groups who can appreciate that electric instruments are more than just ordinary instruments with amplification," Peter Jenner told *Disc and Music Echo* in July 1967. Their approach to sound was placing new textures before a mainstream audience, and the title of the fourth track on their debut LP is a nod to one of Syd's most unusual influences.

The song is called 'Flaming', the lyric doesn't mention flaming so, in that continuing search some choose to make for druggie references, this has been tagged as a term associated with acid culture. "I'm not familiar with it," said Hoppy when I asked him. "I thought flaming was something that came in with the internet, but what do I know?" I'd say it's an homage to a title, rather than a drug.

Keith Rowe has been part of the improvising group AMM since the mid-60s. Despite his modesty, he says: "If you listen to 'Later During a Flaming Riviera Sunset' from the AMM Elektra album [*AMMMUSIC 1966*], there's parts of that which are very much like the introduction on 'Flaming'. It seemed like too much of a coincidence for it not to have been a kind of reference. They do this uncharacteristic, almost ambient sound, very AMM-ish and then it goes into the rhythm. People come up to me and say they've read certain articles or books about my influence on Barrett. I never know what to say about that, as there's only one person who knows and he's not gonna talk about it! What Syd does is take something, perhaps, from AMM or myself and I think the most you can say about it is that he was inspired and it gave him the confidence to do something different."

Compared to 1967, today's music industry is an entirely altered world. A new signing to a major label would now be subject to the opinions of researchers armed with tedious data about market trends and demographics relating to every aspect of sound and image. The magic of an album like *Piper* lies in adventure and unselfconscious joy as the boundaries of 'pop' were redefined. In hindsight, Nick Mason says: "At the time of *Piper*, we were heading down the *Top of the Pops* road: we wanted to be a rock band, rather than make Modern Music."

When Pink Floyd were interviewed for Canadian radio as the next big thing, Syd Barrett said: "It's not like jazz music 'cos . . . " Roger Waters cut in: "We all want to be pop stars, we don't want to be jazz musicians!" and Syd added: "Yeah! Exactly!" Lest we forget, in 1967 the idea of "rock groups" was fresh and, whether it was Jimi Hendrix or Gene Pitney, to most people it was all still "pop music". Ambition and a strong work ethic united Nick, Rick and Roger. If it hadn't, they'd never have continued in the wake of Syd's departure. But even though Barrett claimed he wanted to be a pop star, Matthew Scurfield feels his objectives differed from the other three: "He didn't come across as ambitious. There was an adventure going on and he was party to that. I don't think he coveted being a star. He didn't have that feeling, he just thought 'This is magic!' and the world that you were in when you were in his company *was* magical." Anna Murray agrees: "He was very carried away by the music and he liked performing but, at the time, I thought he'd be better off as a painter. His temperament suited it better. I was really surprised when he took off into music so hugely. I felt he was swept up and it wasn't necessarily his intention or his driving force. It wasn't apparent to me that it was the most important thing in his life at all."

'Flaming' is a hide-and-seek magic carpet ride to what Aldous Huxley described as "the mind's far continents", with fantastic imagery ("Sitting on a unicorn" / "Travelling by telephone" / "Sleeping on a dandelion" . . .). "Others were touching on it," says Jenny Fabian, "but this seemed to be another world; very child-like; somewhere sweet and innocent; it took you to the places that you'd been to on your trips; and if you didn't trip, it took you to somewhere that, perhaps, you thought was better place than the world you were in. You were either out there in the cosmos, floating, looking around and everything was wonderful and lovely, sort of 2001-ish, or you were running through un-genetically modified fields of flowers and being taken back . . . you were removed from time."

Lyrically, the band was "Streaming through the star-lit skies," but an utterly focused performance in the studio produced 'Flaming' in one single take, shimmering with bells, percussion, Binson Echorec swell, tape echo, even a touch of phasing. EMI's notes show that a vocal overdub took place later, but there's no mention of the speeded up piano, so that must have been recorded at the initial session too.

As available track numbers increased and production values changed in the 1970s, the edge of performance, of bands playing together in the studio, was often lost. Post-production trickery was limited in 1967, as Nick Mason remembers. "A lot of the effects we used on *Piper* tended to be fairly basic things and there was a fair amount of new ideas coming from EMI themselves. The Beatles were using phasing, which was a studio effect — no one had devised a live phasing machine at the time — and a lot of tape echoes were very much studio effects rather than live effects." One important invention was ADT — artificial double tracking — devised by EMI's Ken Townsend. Seamless doubling of vocals is a rare skill, so ADT made it possible to reinforce a single voice and make it sound like two takes blended together. ADT was created in time for The Beatles' *Revolver* and was used on *Piper*, particularly on the mono mixes.

The need for a band to get it right brought an urgency to sessions in the 60s, which is perhaps why the best albums from the period are still so exciting today.

Another component of these records was the unique nature of the studios themselves. Mark Cunningham is author of the book *Good Vibrations — A History of Record Production*: "All the studios at Abbey Road in the 60s had customized consoles built by the EMI engineering department and they were fairly uniform. It was all home engineered stuff. Decca had their own too, and there was this closely guarded secrecy between the engineering departments of one studio and the other about what was on those desks. That secrecy was a lot easier to keep in those days because only the people who had to work on the session would be invited into the control room. You didn't have an engineer from another studio popping in to say 'How's it going?', it wasn't that informal then."

"Every desk would've had the same very basic facilities. The EQ actually had POP or CLASSICAL written on it. The EQ for the pop would've been a lot brighter than the classical, which would've had a more full frequency." Pink Floyd took the step of trying out the CLASSICAL equalization on their POP album... pretty radical at the time, I'm sure!

*   *   *

American buyers had to wait a long time to find 'Astronomy Domine', 'Bike' and 'Flaming' on their copies of

Piper. The tracklist for the September 1967 American LP release ran:

Side 1:
See Emily Play
Pow R Toc H
Take Up Thy Stethoscope and Walk
Lucifer Sam
Matilda Mother

Side 2:
The Scarecrow
The Gnome
Chapter 24
Interstellar Overdrive

'Flaming' was coupled with 'The Gnome' for a single release (U.S. only), coinciding with Pink Floyd's tour of the States.

Of their dealings with record companies, Peter Jenner says, "In terms of the U.K. and Europe it was always fine. America was always difficult. Capitol couldn't see it. You know, 'What is this latest bit of rubbish from England? Oh Christ, it'll give us more grief, so we'll put it out on Tower Records', which was a subsidiary of Capitol Records, the tower in question being the Capitol Tower [label H.Q. in Hollywood]. The main thing Tower Records did was put out Mike Curb records and they did very well with them. He did these really cheap, shitty records for cheap, shitty movies about teen gangs with motorcycles — real 'B' features. It was a very cheapskate operation and it was the beginning of endless problems The Floyd had with Capitol. It started off bad and went on being bad." It should be borne in mind that The Beatles and The Stones had similar problems with American albums which were very different from the U.K. originals. Pink Floyd's American releases went through Capitol for several years. Jenner recalls, "When they finally decided they'd had enough and ditched Capitol — this wasn't with me, this was much later with [manager] Steve O'Rourke — they signed up with Columbia for their next album [which would be *Wish You Were Here*]. Capitol then really sold shed-loads of *Dark Side of the Moon* just to show them they could do it, but by that time they'd lost the act!"

Botched Floyd material was not unique to Capitol/Tower. In 1978, a book of sheet music called *67 Pink Floyd The Early Years*, notating singles and songs from the first two albums, was published in London. In addition to many lyric errors, it also managed to credit such items as 'Stethoscope' and 'Julia Dream' to *George* Waters. Although that is Roger's real first name, this was confusing as he had never used it on any Floyd-related material.

*　　*　　*

Ba boom chi chi
Ba boom chi chi . . .

If the opening of 'Pow R Toc H' reminds me of anything, it's the exotic nocturnal jungle sounds of Martin
Denny. Certainly, this has no precedent in pop.

Doing doing
Doing doing . . .

The title is a piece of word play. "Toc H" comes from
the army signaller's name for the initials T.H. "Toc H"
was also a fellowship organisation for soldiers, founded
near the fields of Flanders in 1915 by the wonderfully
named Rev. Tubby Clayton.

Woo-whoooo . . .

A staple of their live set, and a favourite of Peter Jenner's:
"There was a lot of playing, experimenting and making
funny noises. Anything was possible. That, I think, was
the great thing about the sessions. The mouth noises,
mouth percussion, that was very avant garde-y: it
sounded loopy, but without using tape loops." Although
credited as a group composition, David Gale says,

" 'Pow R Toc H' is very Roger Waters. All the vocal things he was doing, the screams and the clicks, all of that strikes me as Waters trying out various effects that he would later take much further. There's a certain economy to those sounds which is evocative of the man himself. Roger is very amusing and very competitive. He's physically very wiry and, in those days was very good at pool and table tennis and used to beat everybody at everything . . . annoyingly! He had a motorbike and rode me down Long Road, which is a long road, in Cambridge and as we came down the hill he just ducked, exposing me to the full blast of the wind and I almost blew off the fucking bike! That's the sort of thing he found very amusing, indeed it was in a way. He was temperamentally very different from Syd, but the two guys were good pals. 'Pow R Toc H' makes me think of that aspect of Waters' personality." It certainly takes the album in a different direction.

I know that this will sound as though I'm talking to obscurist collectors and vinyl junkies only, but this track highlights the reasons for having the mono version of *Piper*: hear the mono mix of 'Pow R Toc H' and the stereo will forever sound tame. It's worth remembering that mono was still the main format when this album was made and separate sessions were booked for working on individual tracks with band members involved. The whole stereo version was mixed in two sessions, all in one day (18th July 1967) by Norman Smith.

In mono, Syd's guitar creates a wash of subtle colours rising through the rolling drum rhythm, jazzy piano, bass and acoustic rhythm guitar. This is virtually absent in stereo. The real prize in mono is the interplay between Syd's viciously overdriven electric guitar break, Rick's horror movie organ sound and the much more prominent screams and mouth noises, eventually subsiding into Nick's thunderous drums at the close. More goblin than Hobbit, it could be the soundtrack for a sacrificial rite — it's unhinged!

Matthew Scurfield views this as a turning point, not just in the album's running order: "You can see the confusion coming. You get it in the difference between the simplicity of Syd's songs and the complexity of Roger's songs." Andrew King goes further: "There were already more than two strands running in The Pink Floyd that you can see very well. There was the classic Syd songs, then there's the freakout element — very long, unstructured solos when they played live and then there was the mainstream European avant garde art element which Roger was involved in and we all felt involved in. All these strings were running through and sometimes they fitted well, sometimes not so well. Already it was clear that there was a problem: there was a Pink Floyd in the studio and a Pink Floyd doing gigs on the road."

*　　*　　*

21st March 1967 saw Pink Floyd in Studio 3 for two bookings. The 2.30pm start produced four takes of 'Pow R', while the late session completed the fourth of these with overdubs. Around 11pm they took a break and ventured next door to meet The Beatles. Norman Smith arranged this, as one did not casually drop in to a Beatles session. They were working on piano overdubs for 'Lovely Rita Meter Maid' that night and, as Peter Jenner says: "They were definitely in control of their sessions, which impressed us. They were calling the shots." Even as new signings, Pink Floyd were given an unusual degree of control. "In the end," Peter told me, "it was always clear that it was our record."

Paul McCartney heard tracks from *Piper* and told the U.K. music press that they were "knockout". Peter Jenner feels that Paul "helped within EMI without me or any of us knowing it. Certainly, he was very supportive overall of the underground because of his whole scenes with Indica [combined book shop & avant garde gallery] and Barry Miles" [who ran Indica with John Dunbar and Tony Asher].

"We benefited enormously from The Beatles," says Nick Mason. "We'd done some recordings before we went to EMI and we understood the basics of multi-track recording and, as I say, thanks to The Beatles, we probably were given more of an opportunity to learn. I know bands still today who've never been given the opportunity to get their fingers on the control knobs. They were kept absolutely away from the mixing desk, whereas we were absolutely allowed to get involved from the beginning and in that respect Norman was just brilliant, because he let us join in. Some of the studio staff, the engineering department, were extremely disapproving of that. I can remember being spotted editing something for *Saucerful of Secrets* and being really frowned on. Someone went and reported me. Apart from some of the engineering staff, there was a great atmosphere. I say some, because others were enormously helpful."

*   *   *

'Take Up Thy Stethoscope and Walk' closes the first half of the album. It's the first recording of a track credited solely to Roger Waters and, for those whose interest in *Piper* is mainly related to Syd Barrett, it's readily dismissed for that very reason. Yet 'Stethoscope' was not a piece of tokenism or filler material: it had been a staple of Pink Floyd's live set since the London Free School shows and, even in the condensed studio version, was clearly the basis for exciting "freakout" explorations.

With 'Stethoscope' in mind, David Gale said: "There's a kind of wit to titling that is very much Roger. Whereas Syd was very amusing to be with, Roger was a much more active humorist and made gags and, in a sense, was more substantial company. You got a wider variety of social effects from Roger: you got imitations and rudeness and cynicism and displays of physical prowess. Syd was more of a genial laughing sort of fellow."

Roger's mordant wit extends beyond the title. Nine lines beginning "Doctor Doctor" chain a stream of colliding images together: i.e. "gold is lead / choke on bread" or "Jesus bled / pain is red". 'Stethoscope' doesn't offer any clues to where Waters' lyrics would go later. It sounds as though he's trying too hard, but he's unsure what for! The slightly arch delivery of

> *Music seems to help the pain*
> *Seems to motivate the brain*

after the central instrumental section has always suggested the image of a white-coated scientist in a 50s movie to me and I suspect that Mr. Waters displayed a healthy disregard for 'serious' music making when he sang those lines.

Any lyrical weakness is redeemed by the frenzied, yet cogent, central break which leaves me wishing that the whole thing had been allowed to ramble on longer. This exciting, immediate recording was the fifth of six takes put down by the band on 20th March 1967, with vocal overdubs added the same evening. It's Roger's tune and his abstract vocal textures are in evidence, along with straightforward, riffing bass, but the core instrument is Rick's dynamically powerful keyboard. "The organ playing was unbelievably spiritual," says Jenny Fabian. "It was almost like psychedelic church music and the other parts, the drums and the bass, were integral. Dylan's band had Al Kooper on *Blonde on Blonde*, but there was something different about Rick Wright's playing and it would not have been the same sound without that. The organ soared and lifted ones' feelings." Rick's outstanding lead on 'Stethoscope' is underpinned by Nick's loose, compelling drumming and Syd's combination of stabbing rhythm guitar and free improvisation before the vocals return in rising harmony at the end of the song.

Even in the early days, David Gale says, "Syd made tunes and Roger made pop spectacle. He had a tremendous foresight into the extension of optical visual spectacle." What Waters lacked in musical technique, he balanced with an abundance of ideas. When interviewed for Canadian radio, pre-*Piper*, Roger said: "We don't really look upon ourselves as musicians as such, you know, period . . . reading the dots, all that stuff," so it must have amused him to see how rapidly Pink Floyd's music was taken very seriously. Peter Jenner says: "Roger was musically inept and had to be helped along. Not in a condescending way, I think it's amazing how he was able to pick up and take the band after Syd left, given his musical realities. I think he did fantastically to eventually become a singer and a songwriter and the quality of the songs he wrote. I mean, absolutely, hats off to him."

3

Side Break

"**F**ront Cover Photo: Vic Singh" said the notes of the Clarifoil laminated sleeve of my copy of *Piper*. I often wondered about this Vic Singh, as I never saw his name on other albums and, perhaps because Syd Barrett himself was credited with "Rear Cover Design", I theorised that maybe Vic was as much a swirling, misty, drifting creation as the image itself . . . Not so!

Vic Singh's family history in India could fill a book by itself. In the late 1940s Singh's parents moved to the U.K. in time for Vic to start school, but even before then he had more important lessons from his father: when Vic was four, he was shown how to develop and print film. When they arrived in England, Vic's mother (the daughter of a Viennese society photographer) worked in a studio and the path was clear: "It was a natural thing since I was a child," Vic says. "It's probably similar to a musician growing up when his parents are musicians."

Vic had several jobs as a photographer's assistant in London, ending up at Studio 5 with other young hopefuls like David Bailey and Norman Eales. Fed up with a low rent lifestyle in what was clearly a high profit business, they asked for a pay rise. They didn't get it, so they left. Bailey and Eales went to work for *Vogue*; Singh — aided by a loan from superstar hairdresser Vidal Sassoon — opened his own studio in Bourdon Place, just behind Bond St. in London's West End.

Among Vic's friends was a young model, Patti Boyd. After she married George Harrison, Vic remembers, "I used to go to lunch in Esher with Patti and George — we were just mates — and one Sunday, as I was leaving he said 'Oh, this is for you. I've got this lens and I don't know what to do with it, so you have it. You might be able to use it for something.' It's a prism lens, it's got facets, so it splits an image up into three or four segments and softens the images because they overlap. A short while later, The Pink Floyd got in touch with me to do a cover. I thought BANG! that lens is perfect for them, it signified them, the kind of psychedelic music and trip they were on. When they came to the studio I said, 'I've got this lens I want to use. There'll be lots of you. It'll be like looking through the eye of a fly.' What I asked them to do was to bring really bright clothes to lift the colour out a bit and I shot two or three reels on a white background. It was perfect for that session and for them at that time. They were so abstract and undefined, transparent. They're very like that lens . . . there, but not there."

Hipgnosis was the design company associated with Pink Floyd artwork from *A Saucerful of Secrets* onwards. Among those involved were Aubrey "Po" Powell, David Gale, Matthew Scurfield, "Ponji" Robinson and Storm Thorgerson, who has also re-packaged *Piper* twice. The first time was towards the end of 1973 when the double album set *A Nice Pair* was issued, presumably to capitalize on the interest in the band's back catalogue following the global success of *Dark Side of the Moon*. *A Nice Pair* simply coupled *Piper* and *Saucerful* in a gatefold sleeve. "We thought it was a bit of a swizz, really," says Storm. "I mean, these albums had already been out. It probably was a cynical ploy, but it seemed really stupid to me. I think Roger called it *A Nice Pair*, with a slightly droll sarcasm, very un-cosmic really — a nice pair of what? Depending on your hormones, it could be a nice pair of boobs or it could be a nice pair of boots! I think we were going to do something about nice pairs, but ran out of jokes. But we did a bird in the hand is worth two in the bush, which is also a picture of a nice pair, but we put one bird in the bush and not two in the hand and that's confusing the issues quite a lot! We thought it was jolly funny — slightly schoolboy-ish stuff really — so we did a couple more and then a couple more, until we ended up with eighteen of these jokes; aphorisms; little conundrums; some chauvinism. We did a picture of a nice pair, then took it much further."

This time around, the botched running order of the U.S. version of *Piper* was replaced by the correct titles in their intended sequence. I say titles rather than tracks . . . as previously mentioned, 'Astronomy Domine' was one of three songs dropped for the original Tower pressing of the LP in the States, but Capitol didn't get it quite right at the second attempt either. Instead of the 1967 version of the opening cut, Americans who bought *A Nice Pair* were treated to the Barrett-less live take of 'Astronomy Domine', lifted from the 1969 set *Ummagumma*.

The Piper at the Gates of Dawn appeared in remastered form on CD in 1994, with a subsequent re-issue of the mono mix in 1997 on both CD and vinyl, marking the 30th anniversary of the album. The audiophile grade mono LP was also part of a vinyl series marking EMI's centenary.

Vic Singh's photo and Syd's design for the rear of the album were augmented by more images. "That was solely to do with lyrics," says Storm. "We didn't do anything to the front, other than add a little pinkness to the letters. When you change the package from vinyl to CD, you obviously alter its size and you add a booklet. Some designers claim it's a challenge to design for a CD. I'm not quite sure what they mean by that, because the booklet, cover, whole damn thing, is generally too small to see anyhow! But this gave us a chance to put all the lyrics on. These are Syd's whimsical lyrics which hadn't had much of an airing, so it seemed like a perfect opportunity. We tried to illustrate each song . . . a bit. There's a mixture of drawings and quite a lot of characters from the songs. This is an attempt in part to illustrate the band in psychedelic days and some not too subtle references as backgrounds to the lyrics. There's a star swirl for 'Astronomy Domine'; 'Lucifer Sam' is a cat . . . interspersed with pictures of the chaps from way back then."

4

Side Two

"**I** think our records will be very different from
our stage shows . . . inevitably," Peter Jenner told a Canadian radio reporter a few weeks before Pink Floyd
signed to EMI. He went on: "Firstly there's a three
minute limitation, secondly you can't sort of walk
around the kitchen humming to The Pink Floyd. I
mean, if you had the sort of sound they're making in
the clubs coming over the radio while you were doing
the washing up, you'd probably scream! I suspect that
our records are bound to have to be much more
audio . . . they are written for a different situation. Listening to a gramophone record in your home or on the
radio is very different from going into a club or into a
theatre and watching a stage show. We think we can
do both." Thirty five years later, Peter said: "A lot of
their live gigs would be considered self-indulgent waffle
if you went to hear them now: the most appalling self-

indulgent waffle, unless you'd taken plenty of drugs. You know, a bit like dance music now!"

By 1967, the sounds you might hear on the radio while washing up were reaching new realms. Thanks to The Beatles and The Byrds, the mind-expanding influences of Ravi Shankar and John Coltrane permeated the mainstream within tight pop song structures. However, the album format was becoming the home for lengthening durations, moving towards a distinct new market. Love's *Da Capo* had the side-long 'Revelations'; there was 'East-West' by The Butterfield Blues Band; The Chambers Brothers scored a U.S. Top Twenty hit with an edited version of their eleven minute invitation to psychedelicize your soul, 'Time Has Come Today'; even The Rolling Stones broke their normally concise limits with eleven minutes of 'Going Home' on *Between the Buttons*.

The six tracks on side one of *Piper* brought fresh, exciting textures, but the biggest surprise awaited listeners who didn't know Pink Floyd's live work over on side two: an extended blues jam is one thing; an organic free improvisation number is another entirely and Norman Smith was ready to let one be heard. Peter Jenner: "It was definitely the deal that — hey, here you can do 'Interstellar Overdrive', you can do what you like, you can do your weird shit. So 'Interstellar Overdrive' was the weird shit . . . and again, hats off to Norman for letting them do that."

More than any other track, 'Interstellar Overdrive' highlights the dichotomy of Pink Floyd. It was the anthem of the underground set at the UFO club; taken on the road, where crowds expected pop hits (and maybe knew only 'See Emily Play'), this jagged musical landscape certainly opened the minds of some audiences to new ideas, but for many others it was a confusing, disturbing catalyst for a hail of missiles directed at the band.

Peter Jenner remembers how Syd Barrett hit upon the central riff: "I tell the eternal story (and my recollection is probably a complete lie by now) but my feeling is that I said to Syd, 'Hey, there's this great song by Love I've just heard — it went like this . . . ' I hummed it and because my singing was so spectacularly out of time, out of tune and all the rest of it, he said 'Is it like this?' and when he played it, it came out as a different song and that was 'Interstellar Overdrive'." The irony is that this skewed inspiration did not come from one of Arthur Lee's own songs: Jenner hummed Love's cover version of the Burt Bacharach / Hal David tune 'My Little Red Book', which first appeared in the movie soundtrack of *What's New Pussycat?* "Love were quite influential, we all liked Love," remembers Jenner.

"Imagine singing that out of tune. It shifted pitch and got squashed!"

The downward progression that is 'Interstellar"s opening theme has a beautiful simplicity to it. Even if (like myself) you're not happy changing chords on a guitar, you can play this: start at b — seven frets up on the e string — and descend fret by fret. Like the most direct ideas, of course, the truly inspired part is that nobody thought of it before! This riff subsides into a five note bass figure which acts as a springboard to freeform "intuitive groove".

Several versions of 'Interstellar' are extant in addition to the finished album cut — far more than any other piece from Pink Floyd's early days. There are alternate mixes and edits of the EMI recording, live tapes and two earlier studio recordings. They chart the development of an innate understanding between four individuals and the best of them, by far, provides an interesting link to a key event in underground culture.

*   *   *

May 1965. Allen Ginsberg arrives in London. Barry Miles' shop Better Books (Earlham Street residents David Gale and John Whiteley work there) becomes his base of operations. Soon, there's a very successful reading at the shop and another, bigger event is suggested.

American filmmaker Barbara Rubin, who Ginsberg knows through his connections with Bob Dylan, moves fast and books the Royal Albert Hall. With only ten days to go, there's an ambitious publicity campaign as poets' names are added to the bill. Hoppy takes photos and makes flyers which say "Come in fancy dress, come with flowers, come!" and on June 11th they do: thousands of them!

The International Poetry Incarnation, compered by Alex Trocchi (who later shared a Hampstead flat with John Whiteley), ran for several hours and included many readings which were less than inspired. In Barry Miles' biography *Ginsberg*, he says "the reading itself was something of a flop," but it "served as a model for big international poetry festivals" and "acted as a catalyst for the burgeoning London arts community, and such diverse organisations as *International Times* and the Arts Lab, a multi-media arts centre for experimental films, avant garde theatre, and performance work; both traced their origins back to the Albert Hall reading."

Jenny Fabian was there: "The London underground scene was very much kick-started by that. I mean, the bohemians and the poets were all bubbling away anyway and that's the kind of scene I'd gravitated to before the other consciousness started to spread amongst us. I don't know quite how it got there, I don't know if it was the acid. Do you blame everything on the drug or would it have happened anyway? Chicken and the egg, isn't it? *Wholly Communion*, Dylan playing, all these things were coming together and it was a historical time." *Wholly Communion* is the film by Peter Whitehead which features the highlights of that night at the Albert Hall. Whitehead had developed his skill in capturing the moment as a cameraman for Italian TV. A new device made it possible for him to film the poets close up without disturbing their scene: the Éclair silent camera.

Peter had lived in Cambridge for a while, where he'd been aware of Syd Barrett as a painter. As Janacek and Bartok were more to his taste, Pink Floyd meant little to him until their paths crossed again: "I had an affair with Jenny Spires, who was Syd's girlfriend at the time. It was she who then introduced me to Syd in London when I was making *Tonite Let's All Make Love in London*. It was Jenny who kept saying 'your film's a bit odd, a bit weird . . . this music, you should listen to it,' so I went along to UFO and saw them performing. It was then that I decided out of the blue to use Pink Floyd as the music for *Tonite . . .* "

"I think I spent eighty or ninety quid and I took them into [Sound Techniques], principally to record 'Interstellar Overdrive', which I intended to use at the beginning and end of my film. We had so much time left, they said 'Shall we do something else?' They then improvised 'Nick's Boogie' absolutely on the spur of the moment." A short edit of 'Interstellar' appeared on the soundtrack LP for the movie, and both pieces have been issued at full length in various formats since 1991. Peter's "eighty or ninety quid" was quite a bargain, especially as the session was recorded by that soon-to-be-legendary alliance of engineer John Wood and producer Joe Boyd.

The studio booking began at 8am on 11th January 1967. There's no record of take numbers, but Whitehead's film of the session intercuts footage of Syd using both a Danelectro and his famous Esquire Telecaster, decorated with mirrors. In some shots, Rick's Farfisa has a Binson on top; in others a half bottle of whisky! There is no artifice for the camera here. The closest to any rock posturing sees Roger pouting as he wrings some final notes from his Rickenbacker before Syd slumps over his guitar and a blue wreath of smoke encircles his head.

Concentration is palpable, as is communication between the four. "I didn't feel there was any principal force there," says Whitehead, "they were just completely welded together, just like a jazz group. I considered it to be pop-jazz, especially when they did 'Nick's Boogie'. Obviously Syd was very beautiful and clearly the guy up front pulling all the girls and was, I thought, gonna be the principal voice in the thing. But I felt there was a feeling between them: that they could communicate absolutely at any given moment. They almost went into trance when they were playing. It was jazz, but they were using a different sound."

AMM's Keith Rowe watched Peter Whitehead's Floyd film, *London '66 – '67*, particularly the close ups of Syd's playing: "They're fairly explicit in the sense of his experimenting with bits of metal. He was obviously experimenting roughly along the same lines as we were, except that he wasn't prepared to put the guitar flat!" The film and the recordings were a thrilling discovery. These are essential items for Syd Barrett and Pink Floyd fans: the perfect complement to the *Piper* album.

*   *   *

Pink Floyd's first recording of 'Interstellar Overdrive' took place around Hallowe'en 1966 at a home studio in Hemel Hempstead, Hertfordshire. The strongest feature of this crude, but still exciting, version is Syd's surf guitar style intro: very Dick Dale! The difference between this and the Sound Techniques session is marked: in the space of a mere ten weeks, Pink Floyd's sense of dynamics and subtlety had reached new heights — and Nick Mason had abandoned "boom-chugga-boom" beat group drumming in favour of a lighter, more expressive touch.

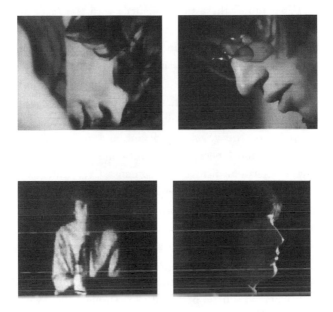

Syd, Roger, Nick and Rick (clockwise from top left) captured
on film by Peter Whitehead at Sound Techniques Studios
and reproduced here with Peter's permission.

What unites these performances with the *Piper* album track is the sense of live interaction. The buzz of the skins on the drum kit in the EMI recording, caused by vibrations from a nearby amplifier, is something which would not have been acceptable in a later, more clinical era of studio work — or, for that matter, in earlier times. Norman Smith set this in context when he spoke to *Studio Sound* magazine in 1998: "Up until the time when I became a sound engineer, the other engineers would always use screens. Everything was screened off so that the separation was good on each mic, but I didn't like that idea for The Beatles once it had been decided that I was going to record them. I wanted to set them up the way that they looked, in line with their attitude and how they approached things, and it seemed to me that they would be far happier if they were set up in the studio as though they were playing a live gig. I therefore threw all of the screens away, and the Abbey Road management warned me that I was taking a little bit of a chance, but The Beatles performed as they did on stage and although the separation on each mic wasn't terribly good it did contribute to the overall sound. We also got a bit of splashback from the walls and the ambience of the actual studio, and in my view that helped create what the press dubbed the 'Mersey Sound'. I'd receive phone calls and letters from America asking how I managed to get all of that sound on tape." Norman carried this principle forward with Pink Floyd. Dave Harris, who prepared the studio before each session began, says, "I don't recall them being screened off. With four tracks, spill wasn't such an important thing. The mics were fairly close, but we didn't use as many then as we do now."

The standard pattern for putting down basic tracks was to record bass and organ on track 1, and guitar and drums on track 2, thus leaving two free tracks for Syd's lead guitar and a vocal. Pink Floyd recorded two takes of 'Interstellar Overdrive' during their second session for *Piper* on 27th February 1967. They didn't revisit the track until exactly four months later — when their "overdub" consisted of the whole band playing along with a reduction of take two.

The start of 'Interstellar' shows the most obvious difference of all between mono and stereo versions. When Norman Smith created the stereo mix, he missed out a whole layer of organ and guitar right at the beginning. Hearing the mono version for the first time was like opening the curtains to let the light in! The heavily compressed mix creates a much more involving sound throughout and brings a visceral quality, more akin to the Sound Techniques recording. The most interesting feature of the stereo mix is the swirling effect at the end. Turning a studio "panpot" to move a sound freely across the stereo spectrum would become commonplace later; in 1967 it was quite an innovation. Smith achieved the effect by using a device built by Bernard Speight and Dave Harris at EMI. This panpot was part of the revolutionary sound system created for Pink Floyd's *Games for May* concert at London's Queen Elizabeth Hall, and the genesis of the "Azimuth Coordinator", which became a central part of their live shows.

*　　*　　*

Events like *Games for May*, television appearances and press coverage put Pink Floyd's name in the wider public consciousness. Even if you hadn't heard them, you'd probably heard *of* them. Duggie Fields had already seen The Rolling Stones and The Who graduate rapidly from pub gigs to nationwide fame, but he says it seemed to happen even faster for The Floyd. For those who loved the scene at UFO, a moment was about to pass. "The concept was good. We wished to be a self-support-ing, self-contained scene," says Jenny Fabian. "It can't be like that, because once entrepreneurs see what people want to do, they immediately degrade it and it becomes a commercial thing instead of a meaningful thing."

At happenings like UFO, Pink Floyd's fusion of sound and light was taking the clientele to places pop music had never been before. Syd described the feeling for CBC radio: "It's quite a revelation to have people operating something like lights while you're playing as a direct stimulus to what you're playing. It's rather like audience reaction except it's on a higher level: you can respond to it and then the lights will respond back." Jenny Fabian says, "They were very much acid music, although I know that it was really only Syd who was taking it all." For Hoppy, "The feelings and perceptions that I'd associated with acid were easily recalled, whether I was doing acid or not, when The Floyd were playing. It was really a very nice experience with some people lying on the floor, some people dancing on the floor." Jenny Fabian: "Before I got to know them, I was one of those people floating around. I would go near the front of the stage at UFO and I'd be lying on the floor out of it on acid. I was very much into those old black and white movies they would show, then gradually you became aware that the movie had stopped and this group had come on. If it was the cosmic stuff at the beginning, you lay there for a bit longer, but gradually it would haul you to your feet: you would rise up with them as the music got into you." For Jenny, 'Interstellar Overdrive' was the pivotal soundtrack to the experience: "Sometimes if you arrived late and you could hear that noise from a distance, you knew that great feeling about it — My Sound!"

The London fan base had grown with the band. For the world at large, Pink Floyd represented such a culture shock that they might as well have arrived from Mars. Jenny Fabian: "They had a terrible time when they went on tour. Some people had never dreamt of hearing this stuff: who were these idiots? This was the lager crowd. What would they want with that? They'd think these guys were off their trees." In the weeks following the release of *Piper*, Pink Floyd gigged around England and ventured abroad, touring Scandinavia and then Ireland. Their nightmare trip to the U.S. followed in October and November of 1967. The legend of Syd's unwillingness to mime on the Pat Boone show has been told many times in other places. A lesser known anecdote shows that, even in America, the platform for rock — as opposed to pop — music was not yet set. Andrew King remembers Pink Floyd's appearance on a 1940s and 50s crooner's TV show as "utterly bizarre, I couldn't believe it. I'd spent quite a lot of time in America with Peter Jenner in 1960, in what would now be called our gap year, so I knew America, but I was astonished by *The Perry Como Show*. Our performance was confusing, to say the least, for the production team [the band played 'Matilda Mother']. Perry Como had this guest — some ageing Southern fascist — who said, 'You know, Perry, all these kids, you know, sometimes I think they're not so bad.' For this man to say the kids are not so bad, that was considered a pretty extreme opinion, an almost communist outburst on *The Perry Como Show*!"

On their return to the U.K. the band took up a space vacated by The Turtles on a 16 date package tour. Imagine the following, then consider whether The Pink Floyd's subtle synaesthesia really stood much of a chance. In 1967 there was no concept of a band touring their new album. Such coordinated efforts had yet to be devised and these shows were little different from a rock 'n' roll revue of the 50s. The compere was Pete Drummond, one of the DJs on the newly launched BBC Radio 1: "It was a showcase for bands riding on Hendrix, he was the headliner. I think he got half the gate and everybody else was on fixed fees. I think [Jimi's bassist] Noel Redding and the drummer, Mitch Mitchell, were salaried. I was on £25 a night and, apart from Hendrix, I had more money than anybody. Even though [The Floyd] were second headliners on this tour, they weren't earning money. I had to buy food for bands — curry and chips for The Amen Corner when we hit Cardiff. I think The Floyd earned about £20 between them per day, so they weren't that bad."

Also on the bill were The Outer Limits, The Eire Apparent with Henry McCullough on guitar, The Move and The Nice. In spite of the radical difference between Jimi Hendrix and, say, Andy Fairweather Low of Amen Corner, there was a common thread between all the bands as they made the most of their spotlight time on stage, selling their image to the crowd. All except one act. "The Floyd, being The Floyd," says Pete Drummond, "were not interested in promoting themselves. That's why this light show was so bizarre: each one of them could've walked out of the theatre at the end and no one would've recognised them, except for the true fan, who would've gone along specifically, because you couldn't see 'em, they were silhouettes on the stage."

"This tour was all theatres with proscenium arches and curtains. When I went along for the job, the tour manager said, 'we'll pull the curtain after a band finishes their number, we'll be changing gear and then I'll bang twice behind the curtain and that means we're ready'. I said, 'How long will that be?' and he said, 'a couple of minutes between the first and second band, a bit longer — maybe ten minutes — between The Nice and The Floyd,' and I said, 'What am I meant to do for ten minutes . . . play some music?' He says, 'Nah nah nah! You just stand there and do what you do. You're a compere aren't you? Tell a few jokes!' I don't tell jokes, but that's what I had to do and sometimes it was fifteen minutes and the audience saw more of me than they saw of anybody apart from Hendrix! I had to stand there and say: 'It'll be a few minutes before the next band and here in Glasgow, reminds me of the Scotsman who . . . ' and just go into some joke. Nine times out of ten, they'd just shout out 'FUCK OFF!' It was no ego boost for me. Hendrix used to say, 'Did you hear me tonight? I was out the back yelling FUCK OFF! early on in the proceedings.' Yeah, I heard you Jimi. I'm getting that audience so wound up against me that you could be the shit worst player on Earth and they'd love you! Roger Waters — especially Roger — used to come up to me and say, 'I've got a good joke for you today.' I had the salient words of jokes written on my wrist."

When the tour hit Chatham in Kent on December 1st, the local reviewer found it disappointing and didn't recognize the music. A few days later, one M. Buswell had a letter published in the *Chatham Evening Standard*, pointing out that if the critic had listened to *Piper*, the live show would not have been such a mystery. The band's set for the tour consisted of 'Interstellar Over- drive' and a new number, 'Set the Controls for the Heart of the Sun'.

Pete Drummond: "There was a split in the audience. Some people had come along to see Hendrix, the pro- gressives, and obviously they appreciated The Nice and The Floyd (they weren't too sure about The Move as they were a bit showy and dressy) and of course there were the young screamers, they were there too."

The Glasgow venue on the tour was Green's Play- house. Renamed The Apollo in the 70s, this became a favourite venue for live recordings by the likes of Roxy Music and David Bowie, who loved the atmosphere.

The Hendrix tour closed there on December 5th. The atmosphere that night was mixed, to say the least.

Arthur McWilliams, a keen guitarist and local band member, was there. "They were a strange act to be appearing on that bill: they didn't fit in. Their appearance was very different to everyone else that night, they dressed very 'flower power' and also the light show was disappointing. The press they'd been getting in *Melody Maker* and *Disc* really featured on this light show more than the music, but because there were so many people on the bill, they didn't have their own light show, so all it consisted of was the fixed spotlights in the theatre while two girls, who seemed to be part of their team, flashed coloured papers over them. That was the light show." Also in the audience was Stewart Cruickshank, who would later become a music radio producer at the BBC: "Pink Floyd had been on *Top of the Pops*, but they didn't play either of their singles and that surprised some of the audience, who weren't sophisticated enough to take all that in. Although there were screaming girls there for the likes of The Amen Corner, the audience that turned up to see Pink Floyd and Hendrix were not a teenybop audience. There were older people, young kids and people in their teens. It was an audience that, within a few months, would be sitting down on floors listening to bands. Syd Barrett and the whole band playing to the max, wild polyrhythmic drums, bleepy guitars and a mantric vocal: absolutely fantastic! Took you on a trip to the moon without being on booze, drugs or anything."

Arthur McWilliams remembers it as "a very educational concert. It opened the audience up to a very wide range of music, in particular music that was confined to London clubs. The majority of the audience that night wouldn't have had the foggiest idea who The Floyd were, but they didn't react against them."

There were two shows that evening: 6.15 & 8.45 pm. The crowd that Stewart was a part of were less accommodating to Pink Floyd. "Up front — bikers, hell's angels, they don't like that, they don't want that. There was a general feeling of unrest and anticipation. They knew that Hendrix was going to be a heavy duty performance. The Floyd were getting pelted with beer glasses — and in those days it wasn't plastic cups. This was a sit down audience, by and large, but they were standing up at the front howling cat calls and pelting them with whatever they had. Pink Floyd left their guitars feeding back and what I remember is this reverberation right round the room and suddenly somebody cuts the power — silence. This is a mighty band, but it can be silenced by the flick of a switch."

Nick Mason: "That tour was fairly tight in terms of what we played. We were limited to twenty minutes, so we played fairly short, tight pieces. Generally, we were doing hour to hour and a half sets elsewhere, so God knows what that would've been like if we'd done that. We could clear ballrooms in no time flat!"

Stewart Cruickshank: "What paved the way for me to 'Interstellar Overdrive' was 'Eight Miles High' by the Byrds, with stunning atonal guitars and sideswerves. We had no direct experience of UFO, you read about these things and what we saw at Green's was a touch of that. It summed up the spirit of the age: just take the music forward, even if the bikers up front hate it with a vengeance!"

*   *   *

"What really struck me about the record overall," says David Gale, "is the extraordinary contrast between psychedelic saga pieces and the much more whimsical stuff which, at that point, was Syd's main input: all the stuff about goblins, gnomes, scarecrows and bicycles — the strong sense of the nursery that those songs brought with them. You're getting two albums for one: the dark side of Syd and the more psychedelic pomp of Roger Waters, plus Waters' drier, less whimsical wit. You're getting these plus Syd's Hobbit / gnomish thing, which places the record usefully as a marker of the vast divisions in the culture of the 1960s. This split I'm describing isn't simply a split between Syd and Roger."

An early idea to record linking passages and segue the tracks on *Piper* didn't get very far. However the meeting of the first two tracks on the album's second side, spliced together without a break, is surely the sharpest illustration of those "extraordinary contrasts". 'Interstellar Overdrive' spirals downwards to close with a sweeping bass drone and an angular rhythm that sounds like distant footsteps, then cuts sharply to the upbeat tick-tock woodblock intro of 'The Gnome'.

> *I want to tell you a story*
> *'Bout a little man if I can . . .*

"I suppose I'm a sentimental old git," says Matthew Scurfield, "but I loved 'The Gnome'. Those simple songs he did were pure Syd. Lots of people felt *The Lord of the Rings* was politically a bit suspect, but it was a big thing for Syd. And *The Golden Bough* . . . " Scottish anthropologist Sir James George Frazer's massive study of folklore, religion and mythology would have appealed to Barrett on several levels, particularly Frazer's research into medieval tree worship and sections like "Beneficial Powers of Tree Spirits". Matthew says that, for Syd "the trees would come alive — really alive — and have characters and personalities for him and that's all in those little songs."

> *Look at the sky, look at the river*
> *Isn't it good*

Some could call it an escapist world, but surely 'The Gnome' reflects Syd's imaginary inner life and strong identity with natural beauty, whether it was found in Grantchester Meadows, a childhood haunt on the banks of the river Cam, or in central London. Anna Murray spent a lot of time with Syd when they both lived in Earlham Street. The fact that they were purely friends, with no other pressures, led to a particularly relaxed link between them: "I had this very individual relationship with Syd. We used to meet up and spend time hanging out on our own and music hardly ever came up." Anna describes a typical day: "Getting stoned, for a start. Go to the park, go for walks, look at trees. He loved trees. I went to art galleries with him. We used to go and look and paintings and we'd talk about art quite a bit. He was very interested in mythology."

I've often heard narrow opinions expressed on everything from Wordsworth's ode to golden daffodils to *The Magic Roundabout*, suggesting that a colourful imagination is created by the consumption of assorted substances. The myth that drugs *create* talent is, of course, the sort of nonsense usually put around by people who have no imagination themselves! As Jenny Fabian says, "Acid can't make something that isn't there, but it can enhance or bring to life things that perhaps were dormant or you weren't bold enough to say, because it releases a lot of inhibitions as well."

Within the contemporary music scene, the closest thing to Syd's way of thinking lay in the songs of The Incredible String Band: Robin Williamson's 'Witches Hat', and 'The Hedgehog Song' by Mike Heron. Joe Boyd, who produced ISB records, said the only person he'd met who was on a similar wavelength to Syd was Robin Williamson, and Hoppy agrees that 'The Gnome' and Barrett's fondness for Tolkien "fit in a loose way with the Incredible String Band's lyrics. Some of Syd's words remind me of ISB, not so much the tonalities, but the words."

'The Gnome' was recorded quickly. David Parker's meticulous research of EMI's archives for his book *Random Precision* turned up some confusing paperwork: was there one take or six? What seems fairly clear is that the basic track, plus overdubs, were all achieved on 19th March 1967. The arrangement here benefits from sparseness. Syd's lead vocal is complemented by Roger's melodic bass line, acoustic rhythm guitar and Nick's swinging woodblocks. Harmony vocals and Rick's celeste playing add a touch of magic.

The celeste, which looks like a small upright piano, brings the memorable tinkling music box quality to Buddy Holly's 'Everyday'. John Cale played it on 'Sunday Morning' by the Velvet Underground and on Nick Drake's 'Northern Sky', but it is usually found in colourful orchestral works by the likes of Vaughan Williams or Tchaikovsky (famously, the latter's 'Dance of the Sugarplum Fairy'). Nick Mason says, "EMI actually had a large quantity of instruments that belonged to the studio. They had glockenspiels, timpani, curious keyboard instruments, so to some extent there'd be a thing of scouring the building, seeing what there was and seeing whether we could use it. Things like the celeste were left in the studio from a previous session and it just seemed like an opportunity to be seized. There's a sort of random air to *Piper*, which is just based on what was around at the time."

*   *   *

The spirit of adventure shared by Pink Floyd and their producer had been described by Norman Smith as a "perfect marriage". In later years, Smith became, shall we say, less effusive. Interviewed by *Studio Sound* magazine, he said, "As musicians, the Floyd were capable enough, but again Nick Mason would be the first to agree that he was no kind of technical drummer. In fact I remember recording a number — I can't now recall which one — and there had to be a drum roll, and he didn't have a clue what to do. So, I had to do that. Nick was no threat to Buddy Rich. Roger Waters, on the other hand, was an adequate bass player, but to be honest he used to make more interesting noises with his mouth.

He had a ridiculous repertoire of mouth noises, and we used that on one or two things; you know, a bit of Rolf Harris." Did Norman play a drum roll? I asked Nick Mason: "Yes he did, but I can't remember where." And what of Peter Bown's claim that an orchestral timpanist was brought in for 'Pow R Toc H'? Nick says: "No — pure invention."

In the pop press of 1967, Rick Wright was often described as "the quiet one in the band" and this non-demonstrative side of his character would lead to his marginalisation within Pink Floyd in more turbulent times. Peter Jenner says, "The great unsung hero [of the *Piper* sessions], in the studio especially, was Rick. He had a lot more to do with the sound than people have ever given him credit for, that Farfisa and all the pedal notes and sustaining chords he used going through all the stuff combined with the echoes from Syd, who was always much more sparkly. Rick was the musical backbone. He was the one who could help find the harmonies, who could sing in tune, who could tell what notes they should be playing. He helped on the writing and he was also very important in helping link Norman to the band as well. Rick knew what a chord was, he knew what a correct harmony was and what was an incorrect harmony. Syd was intuitive. Nick, when all's said and done, was not a very good drummer, but was a very good Pink Floyd drummer, I mean to develop his skills, to do what he did. Again, he was absolutely part of the flavour. You can't imagine The Pink Floyd without those tom-toms and the beaters, that's the sound. That's what's so extraordinary: within all their capabilities and limitations, it's how it all worked. Roger kept his bass lines very simple, backed by those pedal notes and then Nick would be playing the tom-toms, so that gave it that sort of tribal feel. It was a reflection of using what they had, I mean, they were amateurs!"

There had been a prevalent snobbery amongst trad jazz fans, as the vogue for their scene passed and the beat group era dawned. Cries of "They can't play their instruments!" were heard across the land. By 1967, the words "classically trained" began to mean something in pop music with the emergence of bands like The Nice. At the BBC, for example, audition panels gave harsh judgments on the lack of "chops" displayed by hopeful unknowns such as David Bowie or Marc Bolan. Time, however, has shown the importance of fresh ideas over technique. Bowie and Bolan still sound vital, whereas triple albums by "classically trained" prog wizards have long lost their appeal.

For Keith Rowe of AMM, the way he played was an artistic decision based on "coming from an art school background and realising the importance of Marcel Duchamp in the sense that maybe all culture has to go through that gate, being willing to give up the idea of technique. In consequence of that, you have to give up certain ideas about your ego and wanting to prove to people that you can play. AMM were almost the only group who did that. Free jazz musicians were always heavily laden — and still are — with this idea of displaying technique." Pink Floyd didn't have to jump that hurdle, as there wasn't a lot of formal technique to get rid of! Peter Whitehead recalls that this made them all the more exciting: "I heard the Soft Machine, who were more jazzy, but I liked the roughness, the edginess of The Floyd, their ability to take risks and say 'fuck all that! I'm not interested in twelve bars of this or that, I can do anything I like' — and at that time, that was pretty amazing."

To anyone who might carp at the lack of musicianship within the early Pink Floyd, I would suggest some imaginary substitutions. Try, for example, swapping Floyd members with their opposite numbers in The Nice. Lee Jackson was much more technically gifted than Roger Waters, and Keith Emerson's keyboard skills were hard to beat in terms of flash and panache, but either of these components would have destroyed the chemistry within Pink Floyd.

In spite of their unity in performance, it was Barrett who caught most of the attention. "Syd wrote most of the songs," says Jenny Fabian, "so you were aware that it was his projection." Duggie Fields: "Syd was a very domineering presence on stage and he was a very domineering guitarist in that he was the unpredictable one, you were always waiting for him. He was definitely the lead in that way." It's worth noting that Peter Jenner and Andrew King decided to lose Pink Floyd and continue as Syd Barrett's managers after he and the band parted company. In purely commercial terms, Jenner and King made a huge mistake, but their judgment at the time was understandable.

*   *   *

"K'un chen — Earth over Thunder" — the 24th chapter of one of the world's oldest texts, the *I Ching*, and the inspiration for Syd Barrett's 'Chapter 24'. I have a particular soft spot for this song. There's a version by the duo Electroscope and I was one half of that duo. My friend Gayle (the other member of Electroscope) and I sometimes went to Abbey Road to master new recordings. I can relate to those who speak of the atmosphere the building breathes, as I recall being encouraged to wander round the place by a cutting engineer who had worked there since the 60s. Studio 3 was top of the list of attractions!

'Chapter 24' was one of the new songs Syd Barrett wrote for *Piper*. A few takes were recorded at their second EMI session (the one which produced 'Interstellar Overdrive') and one of these was considered good enough to merit overdubs. Immediately following these, the work was scrapped and a late session on March 15th produced a new master. The sense of textural adventure surely reaches its zenith here, as harmonium and Farfisa entwine in mantric drones while electric piano (I'd guess a Hohner Planet) shimmers behind Syd's lead vocal. Nick's soft mallets create a gentle sound like temple gongs and there's more exotic percussion. As Syd sings "Change return success . . . " the words are underpinned by tubular bells. Layers of harmony play against one another as they repeat "Sunset / Sunrise" while Roger's bass almost seems to sing "aum".

Andrew King has a strong memory of 'Chapter 24': "The desk was very simple compared to what you have now and there was no memory in the mix like everyone takes for granted these days, so each mix was a performance, you had to do everything. Often two people would do the mix together, so there were enough hands changing the knobs and levels. It was an art, a craft, it wasn't just a technical thing: you had to *feel* the mix. I remember Syd and, I think, Pete [Bown] mixing 'Chapter 24'. Syd had very little studio experience then, he wasn't exactly a veteran, but I remember watching his hands on the knobs and I was thinking 'he's like a painter' — and he was a fine painter — ' . . . that's it! He's got it!' That was probably the first time I realised just how good Syd was."

I asked David Gale which songs on *Piper* held a resonance of Syd's early interests. "The most explicit and concrete one would be 'Chapter 24' because that reflects Syd and his peers' fascination with the *I-Ching*, which situates us solidly in a period of the 60s when an interest in Eastern religions was percolating over. A syncretic Eastern religion was being composed in the parlours of Cambridge and other towns in England at that time. The *I-Ching* was seen as quite a subversive text because, in the most fundamental way, it threw you open to chance rather than making you submit to dogma. You appeared to be instrumental in getting the advice that you sought, rather than it simply being handed down to you as a passive consumer. You did, after all, throw the coins and activate and connect with the text. A lot of people were really taken with it; some were even obsessed by it. I don't think Syd was obsessed with it, but it's certainly a book that . . . the more you used it as an oracle or counsellor, the more you seemed to get out of it."

To seek guidance from the *I Ching*, one throws three coins, counting heads as a value of three and tails as two. By throwing the coins six times and drawing a broken or solid line, depending on the number resulting from each throw, a hexagram is constructed. There are 64 possibilities at this stage and each leads to a chapter. As number 24 concerns turning back, the phases of time and finding your true path, it's easy to see it as adumbrative of Syd's future. It's undeniably poignant.

The lighter side of Syd's character could be deceptive. Storm Thorgerson reflects: "He was an arty chap, rather than a practical or sporty kind of chap. He was fairly extrovert, but only on the surface. One was not entirely sure, as we saw later when the surface was cracked, maybe the inside was more vulnerable than it first appeared. We were so consumed with interests that were rather narrow, like chasing girls and going to parties. Some of us were more interested than others in the so called mystical pursuits and quite early on some of our group went to India — I think we were only seventeen at the time — and this formed a part of Syd's life later, to a degree. I think he probably enjoyed the whimsical nature of Eastern mystic stories, although I don't want to do him a disservice. We went to see this Master character called Maharaja Charan Singh Ji, who was very impressive, I have to say. I didn't sign up, but some friends of mine did and Syd wanted to sign up, but was declined as being too young. He was already at Camberwell [Art School]. Maybe the Master was wiser than you think and knew Syd was flirting. It might have served Syd very good: it might have given him some protection against the vicissitudes of the business and the seemingly frail ego."

* * *

Amidst regular gigs during the *Piper* sessions, Pink Floyd headlined the *14 Hour Technicolor Dream* at London's Alexandra Palace. They played 'Astronomy Domine' and 'Pow R Toc H' on BBC Television, where Syd and Roger were interviewed by Hans Keller, a moustachioed archetype of a European musicologist who found their music too loud because he had "grown up in ze string quartet" (*sic*). But the most significant augury of Pink Floyd's future came on 12th May 1967 at London's Queen Elizabeth Hall. The show titled *Games for May* took their audio/visual experience a step further by adding a Periphonic surround-sound system which, Nick Mason recalls, was built "upstairs at Abbey Road". Periphonic theatre set-ups will now use, perhaps, 24 speakers. The 1967 system boasted four channels, like the system which became known as quadrophonic. Dave Harris says, "We had four speakers and people in the projection box with slides which they were pouring paint over, and projecting films on a screen."

The set list included seven tracks which would appear on *Piper* ('Matilda Mother', 'Flaming', 'Scarecrow', 'Bike', 'Pow R Toc H', 'Interstellar Overdrive' and 'Lucifer Sam') along with both sides of their first single, a new song which shared a provisional title with the show, and some atmospheric tapes credited to Roger, Rick and Syd. Rick Wright was living in a flat Andrew King had in London's Richmond Hill. Andrew says, "We had some reel to reel tape recorders that we borrowed from EMI. I can't think that we had any sort of mixing facility. In *Games For May* there were prepared tapes [called 'Tape Dawn', 'Tape Bubbles' and 'Tape Ending'] and a lot of those were done in that flat." Dave Harris: "I was actually on the stage and I had to play these tapes from a Ferrograph tape machine, having had a couple of drinkies because of my nerves. To start the show, the guitar on the tape would come out of the back speakers, so I pressed the button and what did the tape do? It spooled off and wouldn't play! I'm in the dark fumbling around trying to get this tape threaded up again . . . just imagine how I felt. It was all right in the end."

Queen Elizabeth Hall staff were accustomed to more formal concerts. Dave Harris says, "I remember the man from the hall coming up to ask [adopts plummy English accent] 'Excuse me, Sir. Can you please tell me how long the first work will last?' Er . . . dunno . . . could be five minutes — could be twenty-five minutes!" From *International Times* to *The Financial Times*, reviews were enthusiastic but, as Nick Mason remembers, venue management didn't share these good vibes. "We were banned from the hall afterwards. The story is that we were banned not because we'd played too loudly, but because one of our road managers had scattered petals in the auditorium and this was considered to be dangerous!"

*   *   *

The song 'Games for May' was a surefire winner. Only a few days after the show, it was re-titled and recorded as 'See Emily Play'. On release, 'Emily''s flipside 'Scarecrow' offered a foretaste of Pink Floyd's debut LP: later that year it would appear as track four, side two.

'Scarecrow' is a close companion to 'The Gnome', pastoral and evocative of both countryside and — according to David Gale — Syd Barrett's home. "I think Cambridge is a city that supports whimsy more readily than London, because it's one of those museum cities like Bath or Amsterdam that is largely pretty and full of old buildings and the signs of the modern city aren't particularly oppressive. It's quite easy to support a whimsy habit in such a place." But how easy was it to retain that feeling? Matthew Scurfield: "The world we were in was very imaginative; full, like a magic world. It was intimate and it was innocent. Syd had a Pollocks toy theatre at his house [in Cambridge] and I had that too and I shared that with him. It sounds like a 60s cliché now, but you would sit on the floor around a table and he tried to unconsciously retain that intimacy that we found sitting round the floor in Earlham Street or even in his home in Cambridge as the limelight grew bigger. That struggle was beginning to happen. Even though his lyrics still had a sweetness about them, there was a cosmic pain that was being slashed through all the moments."

The black and green scarecrow was sadder than me
But now he's resigned to his fate
'Cause life's not unkind he doesn't mind
He stood in a field where barley grows

'Scarecrow' is another example of a master track cut in one single take, at the end of an overdub session for 'Stethoscope' on March 20th. Nick Mason says the distinctive horse trot rhythm was "just a first attempt using a woodblock — everyone liked the sound." Two days later, 12 string acoustic guitar and the trademark early Floyd sound of the Compact Duo organ were added.

Pathé Pictorial ("Picturing this beautiful world") released a short colour film of 'Scarecrow' in the summer of 1967. As Syd carries a scarecrow aloft and re-plants it in a less lonely spot by the water, I'm struck by the meeting of innocence and sophistication which is summed up by Matthew Scurfield. "It was so nice to be in his presence, just simply in a room. His imagination was so rich and — it sounds so soppy as we're so cynical now — he believed in fairies at the bottom of the garden and other worlds. It was like a middle path between *Alice In Wonderland* and Franz Kafka. In the end, the Kafka side got hold of him."

*   *   *

"I was sleeping in the woods one night . . . when I saw this girl appear before me. That girl is Emily." Nick Kent dates that line from Syd Barrett to May 1967 in his book of essays *The Dark Stuff*. 32 years later, *Mojo* magazine reported that "Emily Young, daughter of Lord Kennet, has been officially outed as the inspiration for . . . 'See Emily Play' ". As I read Emily Young's comment — "I didn't know them well at all, just enough to say 'Hi' or get passed a joint" — I wondered who could make such an "official" proclamation while Mr. Barrett himself remains silent. It reminded me of the traffic warden called Meta who once ticketed Paul McCartney's car then, years later, claimed she'd inspired 'Lovely Rita Meter Maid'.

On the other hand, Syd's friend Anna Murray told me that "Over the years, several people have said to me that 'See Emily Play' was written about me — now I never knew anything about this at the time, and frankly I doubt that it's true, but people have told me it was so, seeming surprised that I didn't know — so make of that what you will." Anna shared a lot of interests and adventures with Syd: "I remember climbing over the railings at London Zoo at night with Syd, and walking all over it, wolves' eyes shining at us in the dark, all the bars of cages lost in the gloomy light, elephants looming in the distance, monkeys chattering — so eerie in the dark. I seem to remember also that Syd shared my sadness and obsession with Guy the Gorilla [a popular character at London Zoo from 1947–78], who sat all day slumped in his cage, so obviously intelligent, so obviously terribly depressed — I think we saw him there that night. I climbed in often at night, but only just this one time with Syd." Purely for conjecture, consider who is the more likely muse for Syd: Anna or Emily?

For the 'Emily' session, Norman Smith took the unusual step of booking time at Sound Techniques — where 'Arnold Layne' was recorded — and working with resident engineer John Wood. Jeff Jarratt acted as tape op, just as he did at Abbey Road. From the second Syd slides a plastic ruler up the fretboard in the intro (another moment Andrew King cites as being inspired by Keith Rowe) to the fadeout on Roger's bass, this is one of *the* great pop singles.

While 'Arnold' had hovered on the verge of the U.K. Top Twenty, 'Emily' was a major success. Andrew King remembers the sour verdict of DJ Pete Murray when Arnold' was reviewed on the BBC's *Juke Box Jury*: " 'The public will not be fooled by this rubbish . . . ' dreadful man! The result of that was that all the radio felt very guilty about the way they'd treated The Pink Floyd, they were obviously gonna be a big thing, so when 'See Emily Play' came out, everyone jumped on it and that enabled it to be a full-on hit."

A glance at *The Guinness Book of British Hit Singles* (which uses the BBC's charts) finds the song peaking at No. 6 in the last week of July. Some papers placed it in the Top Five. Jenny Fabian remembers her feelings: "Initially you think 'Ah! Fantastic! The message is getting through, these are our guys! Look! They've made it!' Then suddenly you start to think, rather like Syd did, that this isn't what we wanted to do in life: be on the commercial conveyor belt. We say he flipped out, became a recluse and is strange for it, but if you think about it, he might be the sanest of us all. The Floyd have kept themselves relatively under control, there've never been too many crap stories about them (apart from the incredible fights and the fallout between Gilmour and Waters more recently), but who wants to be a celebrity? Even if I hear kids speak about it, only the brainless ones think it's the thing to be. Any sensible

EMI cardboard shop display, showing (l to r) Nick, Roger, Syd and Rick, from the author's collection.

ones want the perks without having the fame as such. They realise nowadays that fame isn't necessarily a means to an end: it's something you get stuck with that becomes appalling. I don't think The Floyd set out to be famous. Syd certainly didn't." Welcome to the machine, indeed.

Jenny understands the problems of fame better than most. Her autobiographical novel *Groupie* appeared in 1969. Like *Piper* it spoke with a fresh, unique and honest voice. And like Pink Floyd, it wasn't slow in hitting the headlines. Jenny says, "When *Groupie* came out and I started to read hundreds of things about myself, you start to think 'Who the fuck am I?' In those days it wasn't acceptable to be a celebrity for being unconventional. You were a celebrity because you'd done something heroic. Coming out of the 50s into the 60s, you weren't supposed to be naughty to get famous. We were just hitting that iceberg with people like The Rolling Stones becoming famous for being controversial. It was quite hard to handle when you read stuff about yourself that didn't seem to make any sense to you."

Jenny survived those times and remains a witty, incisive writer. Syd's shell was much less resilient, as Matthew Scurfield reflects: "It's very difficult in the modern world not to be shaken if you try to retain that innocence and keep that childhood world where you can see diamonds in the road. People say 'that's just drugs', but it's not: children have that kind of imagination. As things evolved, that was slowly destroyed in a really painful way."

The Piper at the Gates of Dawn was released by EMI's Columbia imprint on 4th August 1967. I asked Peter Jenner what he remembered of that time. "Nothing! It's really strange. You knew the singles position from *Top of the Pops* and Alan Freeman on [BBC radio's legendary chart show] *Pick of the Pops*. One had that, but the album position one didn't have. No one really cared. The record company cared about album sales, but they didn't care about the chart position particularly. These days, it doesn't matter so much what you sell, what matters is your chart position. But what mattered then was *not* your chart position, but what you sold, and it clearly got off very quickly all round Europe once the album came out. That autumn was when things started getting difficult, so the album in a way got lost in all the accelerating wackiness." *Piper* spent 14 weeks on the U.K. album chart, reaching No. 6.

Jenner had very good reason to be distracted around the release date. Only one week before the album hit the shops, Pink Floyd were booked to record a session for Brian Matthew's *Saturday Club*. The set was not completed. Syd left the BBC studio before they'd even finished the first number.

* * *

"The extent to which one can detect within *The Piper at the Gates of Dawn* both the highs and the lows of the entire decade is a sociological challenge," says David Gale. "Possibly there's a PhD in it? I would venture that you can see some of the dynamics that led the 60s to believe that you could have a revolution based only on culture. The majority of people who were deeply involved in the 60s seemed to believe in cultural revolution. I'm amazed when I look back that all the psychedelic fun was going on against a backdrop of Vietnam, it's an extraordinary contrast. I went to demonstrations and riots in Grosvenor Square, but in Cambridge our priorities were psychedelic adventure, consciousness expansion, the idea that you could get in touch with yourself or God or both through the use of psychedelic drugs. Those ideas were very much to the fore and they were surrounded by beat literature, beat culture in general, jazz and psychedelic pop music, which was one of the few strands that led one out towards what was happening in the rest of the world. People like Country Joe & The Fish and The Doors took a position in relation to Vietnam which drew it to our attention."

Piper's closing track could not have been further removed from America's war in the Far East.

I've got a bike
You can ride it if you like
It's got a basket, a bell that rings
And things to make it look good

Matthew Scurfield: "That song resonates for me. It's so simple on one level, but I went through that. It was such a big thing to get your first bike in Cambridge, because everybody had a bike! It was a big, big deal particularly if it was a good one with a basket and a bell and that's what we had in those days, it wasn't racing bikes."

I first heard *Bike* when I was ten years old. I was drawn to it on another level, in a way unlike any other song. It spoke to me of an individual, solitary sort of child imagining ways to connect. Syd's songs were widely imitated. For example, Birmingham band Idle Race had 'Skeleton and the Roundabout', written by Jeff Lynne in pre-ELO days. Jolly fairground sounds, roundabouts and ghost trains might be potential Barrett subjects, but Lynne's song — like so many other imitators — lacks a genuine voice, sounding arch and false compared to Barrett's work.

Norman Smith was a little puzzled. "There was something about Syd Barrett's songs which was indescribable — nondescript — but obviously had that Barrett magic for an awful lot of people. His songs were interesting as far as I was concerned, but more for the question, 'Well, why the hell did he write that?'. You know, 'What inspired him?' "

Syd is the subject of the first chapter in Jenny Fabian's *Groupie*, disguised as "Ben" from "The Satin Odyssey". She describes the songs as "signals from a freaked-out fairyland, where nothing made sense and everything held meaning." Storm Thorgerson says, "His ability to free-associate verbally was of a different order. He wasn't as verbal or as academic as others, but he had a way with words. There's an elision, an onomatopoeia that occurs when he runs words that have no direct meaning, but they seem to feel alright in the way that he does it. That was an innate skill that developed in him that was not part of the general ambience."

Barrett's followers made conscious efforts to achieve a childlike mind-set in their songs. For Syd, there seemed no need to regress. "That's what made him the genius of it all and that's why we all thought how wonderful he was," says Jenny Fabian. Duggie Fields saw Barrett's rapid ascent: "Syd was a star instantly. He was charismatic, handsome, witty, charming, fun to be around. There was always an entourage and the entourage grew. There would be an incredible number of very attractive women knocking on Syd's door with great regularity. Syd had a girlfriend when I first met him, but a lot of very attractive, very intelligent women behaved very badly and lost their cool around him continuously. I think that started to happen from the minute he started performing." Anna Murray agrees: "Syd was a very charismatic performer . . . beautiful, glowingly so. He used to talk about relationships and how difficult they were. I think he was plagued by women. Too many were after him."

"Beautiful" is a word I've heard frequently from people I've talked to about Syd, regardless of their gender. The qualities he had transcended sexuality. Anna says, "He was a rather androgynous kind of being. Men and women found him very beautiful and attractive, but it wasn't a kind of sexual thing. He was very compelling . . . well, beauty is."

In *Groupie*, Jenny Fabian's music biz males are a largely unpleasant, misogynistic, sometimes brutal bunch — but not "Ben". "He doesn't speak and he's got something on his mind," says Jenny "He's driven by his own artistic motivation. The others all seem to be out for a fuck." On the road with Pink Floyd and several other groups, Pete Drummond found that "the groupie situation was quite strong and The Floyd really were the exception to the rule. They were quiet, middle class and, unlike the others."

'Bike' was the first of a new sort of song from Syd, as his world of natural wonder gave way to darker introspection. 'Jugband Blues' made it onto Pink Floyd's second album, but two other songs, 'Vegetable Man' and 'Scream Thy Last Scream', have never had an official release, although both are widely circulated among fans. As the pressure for a new hit increased, these were not EMI's idea of "chart-bound sounds". The cosmic pain which Matthew Scurfield spoke of would find fuller expression on *The Madcap Laughs* and *Barrett*, Syd's solo albums, but even before *Piper* his internal conflict was evident. "He wasn't very communicative even in those days," says Keith Rowe. "I can't remember our conversations, I just remember the disjointedness. You talked to him as if you were talking over his shoulder, in a way. Even in photographs, there's something about the way he's looking at you which is different. To use a cliché, much more penetrating, looking inside you, but when you look back, it's as if something is clicking away in the back of his head which you're not privy to."

Kevin Ayers: "We met up on a wave of sympathetic feeling, but I never felt I knew the guy. He wasn't there for me and he wasn't there for himself either. He was untouchable, inaccessible. Even when I met him in the early days of The Floyd, I found an open door into the universe. His brainchild, the first album, was absolutely brilliant . . . almost too much. A bit like Hendrix, in the end, too much magic burns you out."

Other forces don't exactly help. Roger Waters spoke of Barrett's acid intake on VH-1's *Legends* programme: "There is no doubt those things are very bad for schizophrenics . . . and there is no doubt that Syd was a schizophrenic."

Pink Floyd began recording 'Bike' on 21st May 1967. Although overdub sessions would continue until late June, this makes it the last basic track to be laid down for *Piper* by nearly six weeks. Around a dozen takes were needed, plus three overdub sessions to complete the song.

"There's something about the way the lyric attaches to the metre in a very satisfying way," Roger Waters said on the BBC's *Crazy Diamond* documentary. "The unpredictability of it, combined with its simplicity, made it so special." The arrangement is an ideal complement to the quirky word patterns. Speeded up piano, harmonium and test bench valve oscillator (the sort of thing Delia Derbyshire used at the BBC's Radiophonic Workshop to realise the *Doctor Who* theme) are where it begins. It ends with everything from Syd's guitar to plucked piano strings and celeste playing to an extraordinary collage of sounds. Nick Mason: "I can't remember exactly whose idea that was, probably between Syd and Norman, and then we just assembled all the sounds from the wonderful EMI effects library. They had a huge cupboard stuffed with tapes of all sorts of weird sounds and I think virtually every sound on that is from the EMI tape library, rather than recorded live." The album closes with the looped sound of a goose, tape-delayed, on a sonic flight into its own echo.

5

The Run-out Groove

"If [Syd] wishes to regain his rightful place in the higher echelons of the music scene he must do something *positive* within the next year. Living in the past is all well and good but even this kind of reverence is short-lived . . . people soon tire of old records, no matter how amazing they may be." This is from *Terrapin*, magazine of the Syd Barrett Appreciation Society. John Steele wrote those words in 1976, concerned that interest was dwindling. His attempt at a Barrett biography foundered when publishers he approached showed no interest. Pink Floyd, with Syd's old friend David Gilmour taking on the role of lead guitarist, had become a global musical phenomenon. Yet, even though Barrett had been out of the band since early 1968, he was far from forgotten. David Gilmour and Roger Waters helped him finish his first solo album. Gilmour was joined by Rick Wright in the production of his second and, even when Syd no longer made records, his life inspired some of Pink Floyd's best known works.

In 2001 Pink Floyd released a double CD called *Echoes*. Of the twenty-six tracks chosen to highlight their entire career, five were written by Syd Barrett and recorded during their first year in the studio. Storm Thorgerson packaged this compilation. "One of the really interesting things about doing *Echoes* was that Syd's material on it has a quality of freshness and chord juxtaposition that was really invigorating. When you hear the record, it tells you quite a lot about The Floyd and how The Floyd became famous. In the same way, *Echoes* tells you something else about The Floyd, which is not about Syd. This freshness is actually very noticeable and is the great thing about *Piper*. It's slightly brash, slightly simplistic, but very fresh. The liveliness and the quirkiness of it wasn't really in The Beatles either."

Echoes opens with 'Astronomy Domine' and closes with 'Bike', just like *Piper*. The material is, therefore, not arranged chronologically and this leads to some sharp contrasts, none more so than near the end of disc two. The song which immediately precedes 'Bike' is 'High Hopes', which contrasts childhood aspirations with the resigned drudgery of unhappy middle age. The irony of this rather depressing slice running headlong into 'Bike' was clearly intentional. Songwriting royalties from platinum sales of *Echoes* help to cushion Roger

Barrett (he stopped using the "Syd" nickname many years ago) from the world. In 2001, Genesis Publications printed *Psychedelic Renegades*, a collectors' album of photographs of Syd Barrett from 1969–71 taken by Mick Rock. Mick was another dweller at 101 Cromwell Road and, thanks to a friendship of long ago, 320 deluxe editions of the book carried an insert signed simply "Barrett". This is Roger Barrett's only voluntary contribution to a work about him. Unlike Peter Green or Brian Wilson, he has shown no interest in becoming a public figure again. As Jenny Fabian says, "Where would Syd have gone through the 70s, 80s and 90s? Would he have become some kind of ancient, ambient trance musician? When you look back, he did absolutely the right thing: he flipped out and disappeared!"

There's no way I could hope to list all the tributes and references to Syd Barrett from musicians and writers other than Pink Floyd. He inspired Kevin Ayers to write the wistful, charming 'Oh! Wot A Dream' for his *Bananamour* album. "I just wrote it because I recognised, you know, one weirdo to another!" says Kevin. Peter Whitehead now writes novels. The best known of his books, *The Risen*, is dedicated to Syd Barrett. Both of these are well worth tracking down and the flow seems unending. During the time of writing, I've heard of a new album coming out on OVNI records in Italy. It's called *The Vegetable Man Project* and features no less than twenty versions of that song by bands from the U.S. & Italy! Who could have imagined that, even with the passage of decades and tides of fashion, even obscure Barrett songs would find new, young fans? Certainly, the appeal of *Piper* extends far beyond mere nostalgia.

"It was Syd's album," says Peter Jenner. "It couldn't have happened without the others, but he was the driving creative force. It just exudes Syd and all his madness and his genius, it's got that magic in it. It's very spontaneous and it has a childlike-ness and a naïvety, which was a function of who they were and where they were, both in terms of their personalities and their career. It's got that freshness of youth and that freshness of discovering things and I think that's something which gives it a unique quality."

Admirers of the album are often divided. To some, it represents the beginning of a great canon of Pink Floyd music. Those who don't care for post-Syd Floyd will identify with Kevin Ayers' thoughts: "There was something magical, but it was all in Syd Barrett. After that, it faded out . . . stopped. They had one amazing album, obviously governed by Syd Barrett and then Pink Floyd became something else totally . . . the most expensive blues band in the world! [*Piper*] was Syd's magic spider's web and I'm sorry about the price he had to pay for it."

BBC producer Stewart Cruickshank: "Even if Pink Floyd had never made another record, people would still talk about them now in much the same way that they'll talk about the first MC5 record, because it captures something. People like Delia Derbyshire and Stockhausen had all experimented in wonderful ways before, but nobody had made it sound quite as tight and launched it into space in terms of popular music. It's pop music of a different order and one which Pink Floyd, despite all their success and — to be fair — some of the great things they came up with later, for me they never caught that again. When *Saucerful of Secrets* came out, I thought it was a wonderful record — it still is. Even if the Barrett contributions hadn't been there, I think it would've been a very forward looking record and then *More* came after that. Wonderful records, but are they as cohesive? Are they as complete and do they have that sense of awe that *The Piper at the Gates of Dawn* has? You know where the reference comes from and the LP lives up that."

Kenneth Grahame's iridescent prose, his words bringing alive a dawn-light meeting of two small animals with the God Pan, is the perfect inspiration for Syd Barrett's choice of album title: "So beautiful and strange and new! Since it was to end so soon, I almost wish I had never heard it. For it has roused a longing in me that is pain, and nothing seems worth while but just to hear that sound once more and go on listening to it for ever . . . "

I have listened to this record countless times across most of my life, but never quite so often as during the work on this book. I've listened to it with contributors; discussed each track; carefully studied the arrangement, production and mix; and played it through to consider the overall effect. Never once have I felt fatigued by it and, if anything, I've come to enjoy it even more than before. And yes, I could quite happily "go on listening to it for ever".